Charles William Hubner

Historical souvenirs of Martin Luther

Charles William Hubner

Historical souvenirs of Martin Luther

ISBN/EAN: 9783337127244

Printed in Europe, USA, Canada, Australia, Japan

Cover: Foto ©ninafisch / pixelio.de

More available books at **www.hansebooks.com**

NAILING THE THESES TO THE CHURCH DOOR.

OF

MARTIN LUTHER.

BY

CHARLES W. HUBNER.

CINCINNATI:
HITCHCOCK AND WALDEN.
NEW YORK:
NELSON AND PHILLIPS.
1873.

Entered, according to Act of Congress, in the year 1872,

BY HITCHCOCK & WALDEN,

In the Office of the Librarian of Congress, at Washington.

PREFACE.

NO study within the range of the human mind is more interesting and instructive, or better qualified to ennoble the soul, than the study of the lives of men who, impelled by the Spirit of God, have devoted their days to the promotion of the spiritual welfare of their race. Such men illumine the era in which they live with a luster far brighter than the splendor of victorious arms. Their imperishable monuments are built upon the affections of the Christian heart; reverence and love attach themselves to their memories with deathless fidelity.

The good they have done is "a thing of beauty and a joy forever," emitting its holy light long after the glory of conquerors and of kings shall have been quenched in the darkness of the past, and their names become undecipherable hieroglyphics upon the crumbling ruins of past ages.

Among the grandest of all the names emblazoned upon the world's roll of honor, appears that of Martin Luther, the Father of the Reformation; the moral hero; the humble, God-fearing man; the mighty warrior of the Cross; the champion of truth, and slayer of the hydra-headed Roman dragon, whose fangs poisoned the life of the world. To place before the reader a brief and truthful sketch of the great reformer's home and public life, as connected with the leading events in that remarkable epoch in the religious history of the world, has been the object of the writer. He believes that many who would shrink from the task of perusing the elaborate and ponderous historical and polemical works referring to this period, will avail themselves of these condensed pages, deriving from their contents at least some of the profit which must accrue from the study of the lives of such men as Luther.

In this spirit, the volume is dedicated to the public by

THE AUTHOR.

Contents.

CHAPTER.		PAGE.
I.	Luther's Birth and Boyhood,	9
II.	Luther an Augustinian Monk,	14
III.	Removal to Wittenberg and Journey to Rome,	17
IV.	Spiritual Struggles and Triumphs,	26
V.	Gross Superstitions of the Age—Luther's Famous "Theses,"	30
VI.	Melanchthon—The Gathering Storm—Cardinal Cajetan,	37
VII.	Luther *vs.* Eck—Luther's Excommunication—He burns the Pope's Bull,	47
VIII.	Luther appears before the Diet at Worms,	54
IX.	Luther waylaid by his Friends—The Wartburg Asylum,	63
X.	Luther leaves the Wartburg—False Prophets,	75

CONTENTS.

CHAPTER.		PAGE.
XI.	LUTHER AS HUSBAND, FATHER, AND FRIEND,	81
XII.	A CHARACTERISTIC LETTER—HIS WIFE AND CHILDREN,	90
XIII.	CHRISTMAS IN LUTHER'S HOME—DEATH OF MAGDALENA,	97
XIV.	LUTHER'S CATECHISM—THE DIET AT SPIRE IN 1529—RESULTS,	104
XV.	YEARS OF TRIAL AND AFFLICTION—LUTHER'S HYMNS,	109
XVI.	DEATH OF LUTHER—HIS FUNERAL—SCENES AND INCIDENTS,	124
XVII.	REMINISCENCES OF WARTBURG AND WITTENBERG,	131
XVIII.	THE LUTHER MONUMENT IN WORMS,	145

ILLUSTRATIONS.

	FACE PAGE
NAILING THE THESES TO THE CHURCH DOOR,	*Frontispiece.*
LUTHER AT ROME,	18
LUTHER LEAVING THE WARTBURG,	76
THE LUTHER MONUMENT AT WORMS,	145

Historical Souvenirs.

CHAPTER I.

LUTHER'S BIRTH AND BOYHOOD.

MARTIN LUTHER was born in the pleasant little town of Eisleben, in the Electorate of Saxony, on the tenth day of November, 1483. He was baptized on the following day, which, happening to be St. Martin's day, furnished his happy parents with a proper baptismal name. His father's name was Hans Luther. He was originally from Moehra, in Thuringia, and followed the arduous occupation of a miner. He was very poor, but was noted for his extreme piety. Luther himself says: "My father was a poor, hard-working miner, and my mother used to gather the fuel necessary for the family in the neighboring woods, and carry the load home upon her back. Both of them worked like slaves for their daily bread."

Happily, an improvement in the condition of the family took place, by reason of the promotion of Hans Luther to the overseership of a brace of furnaces attached to the mines, and the consequent increase of wages was religiously applied by the old man to the education of his little son Martin. He used to carry him to school in his arms, as the child was weak and delicate in body, and the distance from their home to the school-house too great for him to walk. In 1497, when fourteen years old, Martin was sent to the celebrated school at Magdeburg, but in the following year he was removed to the school at Eisenach, in which town several of his mother's friends resided.

Here, as well as at Magdeburg, little Martin, in company with a number of other so-called "pauper scholars," earned a scanty subsistence by singing hymns upon the streets and in the public places of the town. The boy's noble bearing, and the fervent, enthusiastic manner in which he sang his little hymns, attracted the attention of a benevolent and pious lady, the wife of a wealthy citizen named Cotta, who took him into her house. Under her hospitable roof the boy was sheltered and fed for a long time.

After a residence of four years in Eisenach, Martin Luther, in 1502, was allowed to enter the famous University of Erfurt, where his diligence and studious habits, as well as his rapid progress in every branch of human knowledge, excited the wonder of his contemporaries. We shall marvel less at this surprising and gratifying evidence of success in young Luther, when we remember that he never failed to invoke Divine aid and blessing in fervent prayer at the beginning of every day's task. His motto was: "A prayerful spirit smooths the rough path of study, and serves to remove half of its weight."

It was in Erfurt that the young and devout student became possessed of a treasure of far greater value to him than all the riches of the earth could have been to him; namely, the Bible, which, until this time, as he himself says, in one of his letters, he had never seen before. He found the sacred Book in the great library of the University, and at once began to study its divine truths with so much diligence and care, that young Luther soon became noted as a very bright and promising theologian. His parents, however, wanted him to pursue the study of law. A great conflict was going on in the heart of the devout student, and his mind became imbued with the results of continuous meditations upon the "wrath of God, and the terrors of Judgment-day." An incident which occurred to him about this time, also had a deep effect upon his impressible spirit. Going to the room of his college-mate and intimate friend, Alexius, early one morning, he found the latter lying dead upon his bed, murdered by the hand of an assassin. Rushing horror-stricken from the fearful scene into the open air, a sudden flash of lightning blinds his sight momentarily, and an instantaneous crash of thunder causes him to reel senseless to the ground. On recovering from his stupor, the impression made upon his soul by these events was too deep and lasting to be neglected or removed. The imminence of death forced upon him the conviction of the perils attending an unconverted heart, and the urgent necessity for such an one to seek the way to salvation.

CHAPTER II.

LUTHER BECOMES AN AUGUSTINIAN MONK.

BELIEVING that nothing could more effectually contribute to the restoration of his peace of mind than the seclusion and sanctity of a monastery, Luther determined to become a monk; and, in the pursuance of this object, he entered the Convent of St. Augustine, belonging to the order of Dominican monks. This occurred on the 17th of July, 1505, when Luther had entered the twenty-second year of his age. He subjected himself devoutly to all the severe discipline and rigors demanded by the rules of the order. But notwithstanding all the fasting, penance, vigils, and other authorized mortifications of body and soul which he inflicted upon himself systematically, Luther failed to find that peculiar spiritual peace for which he so deeply yearned. He did not then know that this Divine blessing is not attainable simply through works, but exclusively by the grace of God, through faith.

The good counsel and admonitions of an old man and fellow-member of the order, were the first means to direct Luthur into the true path. While the latter was prostrated with sickness, caused by the intensity and severity of his monastic penances, and suffering much mental anguish, his aged friend dispelled much of the gloom that seemed to rest around the soul of the novice, by urging upon his attention the comforting assurances contained in the Holy Scriptures concerning the remission of sins. He also reminded him that, though all men are guilty in the sight of God, yet they are freely justified by his grace, through the redemption in Christ

Jesus; therefore, they who believe in the efficacy of the blood of the Redeemer are justified by faith, without the deeds of the law. The words of his venerable teacher soothed and cheered the troubled soul of Luther, and shed upon his darkened heart the mild glory of an immortal faith. The justification of man through the power of faith, without reference to works, became henceforth the guiding religious principle of Luther's life, by means of which he achieved his most signal triumphs; as he himself says, "I overcame the Pope, and all his doctrine and power."

Having thus been prepared for the important work for which the Divine will had destined him, the same Omniscient Power prepared the means by which Luther was to quit the fruitless solitude of a monk's cell for the rich and illimitable fields of public usefulness.

CHAPTER III.

REMOVAL TO WITTENBERG, AND JOURNEY TO ROME.

FREDERICK, surnamed the Wise, the reigning Elector of Saxony, a few years before this period, had founded the University of Wittenberg. At the request of the elector, Luther accepted a call, and assumed a professorship in the new University. Shortly after this event—that is, in the year 1512—Luther had the title of Doctor of Divinity conferred upon him, and as such took a solemn oath "faithfully to preach and teach, in all purity, the doctrines of Holy Writ, even unto the end of life." This oath he never violated. His devotion to truth, and his loyalty to the Divine precepts of the Bible, never faltered, no matter how great the temptation to infringe upon a strict construction of these principles might have been, or however imminent the danger of personal violence at the hands of his foes, to which he rendered himself liable.

In the year 1510, Luther visited Rome on business connected with the order of Augustinian monks, of which he was still a prominent member. During his residence in the "Eternal City," the observant German monk had abundant opportunities to witness the depravity of the Roman priesthood, and the unbounded corruption of the Pope and his hierarchy.

Speaking of this journey, Luther says, "I would not take a hundred thousand florins for all that I have learned while in Rome."

In fact, this pilgrimage of Luther to the footstool of the Holy Father was of incalculable value in its consequences. The facts

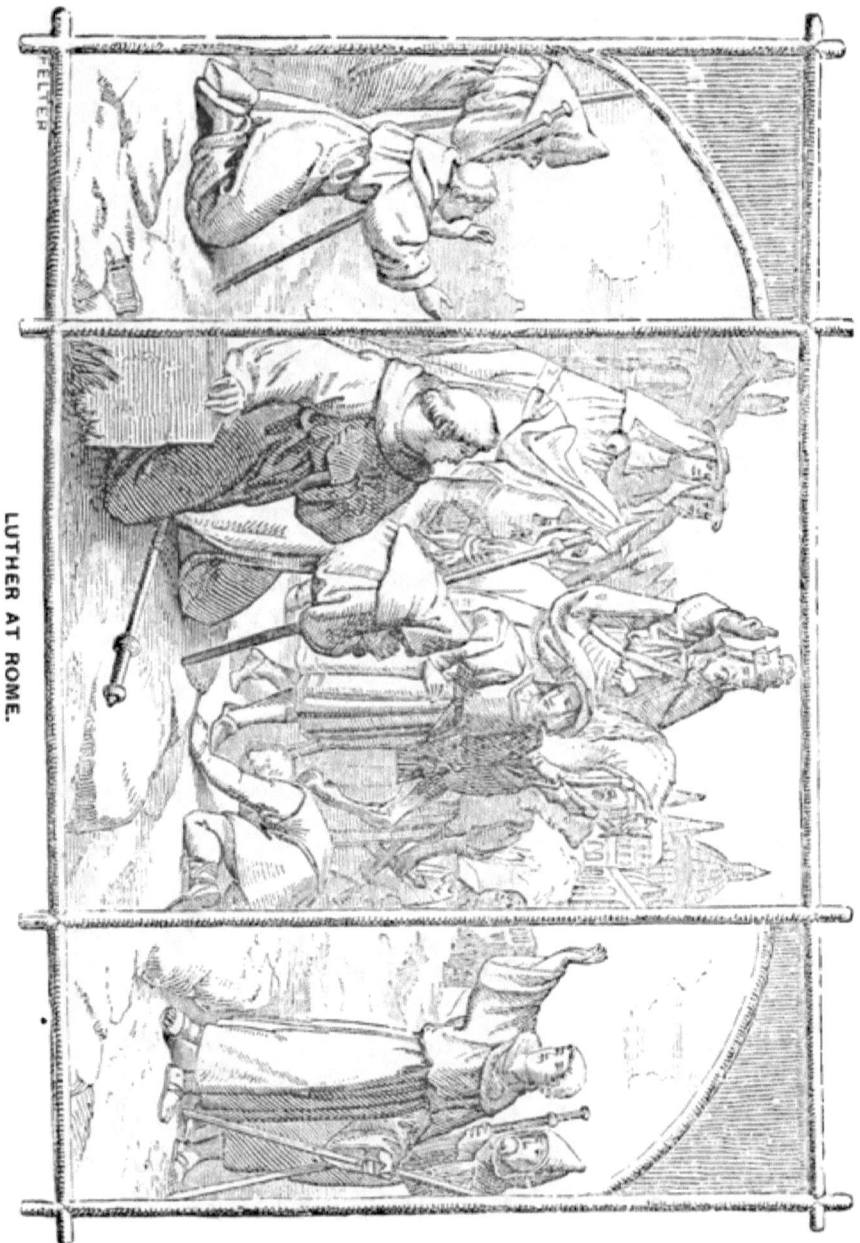

LUTHER AT ROME.

gathered in this great reservoir of Papal iniquities, contributed largely toward the perfection of those foundations of the true faith upon which the Great Reformer thereafter stood, immovable under the frowns of prelates and of kings, unaffected by the thunders of the Vatican or the threats of instant death. It nerved his strong arm in defense of Gospel truth, and added keenness to the sword of his intellect, wherewith he clove, to the very core, the huge and festering body of intolerance and fanaticism then infecting the world.

Luther undertook the journey to Rome at that time with more than ordinary interest, being engaged, in his duties as professor, in expounding the Epistle of Paul to the Romans; and his inquiring spirit was filled with the importance of that declaration of the inspired writer which says, "The just shall live by faith." (Romans i, 17.) He believed that, by visiting the "Holy City" and its numerous sanctuaries, by pious meditation before its shrines, and other acts of devotion under the shadow of the Chair of St. Peter, he would acquire that quietness of heart and peace of conscience for which he so ardently yearned. He also entertained the prevailing notion of the times, that the nearer a person could live to Rome, the better the favored individual would be in every religious respect, and that to *live* in Rome, the seat of the "Holy Father" himself, must be equivalent to a residence in heaven!

But when Luther, after a long and weary journey, beheld the reality, how great was the deluded man's disappointment! how effectual and complete the disenchantment of the astonished, simple-hearted German priest!

He found that the highest offices in the Church were bought and sold like so many yards of cloth, and the most responsible ecclesiastical positions at the mercy of any hypocritical rascal whose purse happened to be well filled. He found vice, in every conceivable shape, publicly indulged in by a degraded populace, and that in Rome, more than anywhere else, the most shameless profligacy and debauchery obtained among the clergy, of whom but one in a hundred could celebrate mass with a decent degree of Christian solemnity.

Luther says: "I was often present in the churches during mass, and shudder when I remember the sacrilegious proceedings. I was disgusted to see the priests hurrying through the offices of their holy function in such a helter-skelter style, as if the whole thing was a Punch-and-Judy show at a village fair. Before I could get to the Evangelio, they had already rushed to the end of the entire services, and would cry to me, *Passa! passa!*—hurry! hurry!"

Even during meals, he would hear some of the clergy mock at the sanctity of the Lord's-supper. The Pope and the cardinals, whom Luther had supposed he would find to be the most devout and God-fearing of men, he found to be, on the contrary, rather the leaders of heresy, as well as promoters and abettors of a carnal and godless mode of life.

The "infallible" head of the Roman Church at this period was Pope Julius II, who prided himself upon his military achievements, and even led his cohorts in person against the army of Louis XIII of France, with whom he was engaged in a deadly feud concerning the extent and prerogatives of the Pontiff's temporal power.

The predecessor of Julius was Pope Alexander VI, who occupied the Papal throne during the years 1492–1503, and who is notorious in history as one of the most profligate of the occupants of the Vatican, guilty of inexpressible vices, and even the crime of murder. In short, all that Luther saw and experienced, while living in Rome, was wholly contrary to every thing he had expected to find there, and demolished at a blow the entire imaginary fabric of holiness which he had conceived to be visible in the capital of Christendom.

Still urged by the power of hereditary faith, and in his efforts to be a good and orthodox Catholic, Luther strove manfully against these overpowering and disheartening influences. He kept himself actively employed, and, with the view of reviving the dying flame of orthodox Church enthusiasm, he visited habitually the shrines of the saints, and other reputed holy places of the city.

Luther says: "I, too, was one of those mad saints who rush around Rome, and crawl about the churches and miraculous grottoes there, believing all the lies that are told about them. While in Rome, I officiated in the celebration of ten masses, and doubtless, too, would have worked with pleasure in the way of supplications, masses, and other precious acts, to get father and mother out of purgatory, had they been dead instead of living."

His conscience, however, was still unsatisfied, and the doctrine of the remissions of sin perplexed him greatly. Among many other fables dished up by the Roman priests, to stuff the maw of the credulous populace, was the so-called "Staircase of Pilate." This, the priests averred, was the very staircase before the house of Pilate, in Jerusalem, upon which our Savior stood when the Roman Governor presented him to the assembled Jews with the words, "*Ecce homo!*" By a Bull, the Pope had declared that any one who would ascend these miraculous stairs upon his knees, piously muttering a particular prayer upon every step, he or she should have full absolution for all sins, in time and eternity!

Luther, still impressed with the supposed truth and efficacy of these edicts of the Pope, faithfully undertook and accomplished the feat of climbing the wonderful Pilate stairs upon his knees. But it failed to accomplish the result he so fervently anticipated; his heart remained unsatisfied, his yearning spirit unappeased. The doctrine of man's justification through faith remained the constant theme of his meditations. Though the meaning and full bearing of this truth was still clouded, the great principle upon which it is based never forsook his soul. Dissatisfied, and hungering after truth, Luther departed from Rome, after having disposed of the business of his order to the satisfaction of his superiors.

CHAPTER IV.

SPIRITUAL STRUGGLES AND TRIUMPH.

ON his journey home, Luther fell dangerously sick at Bologna, and was overcome, for a time, with a profound melancholy, which threatened to consume him. Nevertheless, the holy and soothing light of the truth and beauty of the Scriptures penetrated the gloom of these sad and evil days, and the power and manifestations of God grew and flourished in his heart. When he had safely returned to Wittenberg, Luther devoted himself with still greater diligence and fervor to the study of the question of man's justification through faith. His soul grew stronger in this propitious spiritual struggle, and the fervency of his belief deepened and broadened, and rose triumphantly higher and higher from day to day, as he succeeded in comprehending the Divine purpose, and held in his firmer grasp the golden chain of meaning extending from the heart of man even unto the throne of the Infinite.

He found that a troubled spirit, and a heart yearning for salvation, can only attain rest and peace by the exercise of child-like trust in the wisdom and beneficence of Jehovah, and by solacing itself with the knowledge that the Lord Jesus Christ died for all men, and that he is the Lamb of God which taketh away the sin of the world. He began to understand, clearly and fully, that man can not encompass the remission of his sins by his own works, but that the sins of every penitent heart are alone forgiven by the grace of God, through the redeeming blood of the Savior, and that this all-sufficient grace can be reached through faith in the Lord Jesus Christ. He comprehended the difference between the Law and the Gospel—how that the Law promulgates inexorable decrees, with the demand "You shall!" whereas the blessed Gospel extends to all men the olive-branch of everlasting peace; drawing man to his Creator, under the direction of the Holy Ghost, and through the persuasion of Mercy and Love; strengthening the soul with the divine power of a living Redeemer, so that God's free grace may enter, and the believer, by means of these instrumentalities, may, through new paths of truth, reach the blissful shore of everlasting life.

Luther, speaking of this eventful epoch in his spiritual life, says: "I felt that I was born again, and that I had discovered a wide and open door, allowing me to penetrate into paradise itself. I viewed the Holy Scriptures in a far different light from what I had formerly done, and through this discovered the true way to everlasting happiness."

Thus we find that this great and noble man

arrived at the state in which his heart was enabled to enjoy the fruition of Gospel truths, firstly, by means of the strictly pious training which he had received, as a child, at the hands of religious and conscientious parents; and, furthermore, by the brave manner in which he bore up under the crosses and burdens of life, by the sincerity of his efforts to secure salvation, and by experiencing the efficacy of repentance, through which he found the peace contained in Christ, and with this peace the new life of the Spirit, "the power of God unto salvation to every one that believeth." In this way, by first renewing and reforming himself, was Luther called and prepared to renew and reform the living Church of Christ.

CHAPTER V.

GROSS SUPERSTITIONS OF THE AGE—LUTHER'S FAMOUS "THESES."

LUTHER was obliged to be extremely cautious in his first endeavors to rid the Church of some of the grossest errors and superstitions then befouling it, and to attack the prejudices industriously fostered by a corrupt priesthood. The ramifications of the evil were so tenaciously intertwined with the life and habits of the people, and the clergy manipulated the feelings and fancies of the ignorant masses so skillfully, to further their own selfish purposes, that a wily study of details, and the utmost circumspection in attack and defense, were essential to insure even the slightest success at reform, — and here again, a happy concatenation of circumstances transpired to assist Luther's design.

Dr. Staupitz, the vicar-general of the order, was compelled, at this time, 1516, to undertake a protracted journey into the Netherlands on official business. He authorized Luther to make the usual annual tour of inspection in his place, among the forty monasteries connected with the order in the principalities of Meissen and Thuringia. In the discharge of this important duty, Luther found every-where the most profound ignorance and turpitude. Religion existed in name, but not in fact. The daily life of the common clergy, and that of their still more degraded parishioners, was spent in a series of fastings, pilgrimages to miraculous shrines, and the idolatrous worship of images. A barbarous, absurd, and vicious system of monkish ritualism had taken complete possession of the public mind. Deeply grieved and mortified at what he saw, Luther endeavored to mitigate these evils by all the means in his power. He established schools, lectured, and preached, and strove by word and deed to inculcate sincere Christian worship, and to impress upon his hearers the necessity of reading the Bible and obeying its laws.

About this time an itinerant "huckster of indulgences," named Tetzel, appeared in the vicinity of Wittenberg. This person's vocation will be understood when it is remembered that the Pope had shamelessly concluded to sell his supposed divine power to remit the sins of the world, to any one who desired to retail that desirable privilege among the faithful. In this manner he made profitable merchandise out of his acknowledged infallibility as the pretended Vicar of God upon earth, and sold the agency at so much a slip to any ecclesiastical huckster who might desire to obtain a livelihood by hawking the Pope's "indulgence grants" around the country. This fellow, Tetzel, was one of the vilest of this herd of Papal "drummers." He harangued crowds upon the highways and every market-place, guaranteeing to every purchaser of his "indulgences," in the name of the Holy Roman Father, complete remission of all sins, past, present, or to come; no matter if the crime committed, or to be committed, be theft, adultery, robbery, or murder. Tetzel proclaimed his motto to be:

> "So bald der Groschen im Kasten klingt
> Die Seele in den Himmel springt!"

which, literally translated, means that as soon as the pennies drop into the money-chest, the soul will go to heaven. This was a sweet and tempting morsel to the vulgar and vicious masses, and great crowds from Wittenberg and the surrounding villages visited Tetzel's booth. Whenever these people appeared before Luther in the confessional, and he began to rebuke them for their wickedness and licentious habits, they would reply to his counsels with the utmost impudence, saying: "We need no confession; because we have the Pope's authority to do as we please. The Holy Father's agent has sold us indulgence. We are released from all penalty for sin, as you call it, now or in the future. Tetzel's papers are sufficient." Luther, incensed at such hypocrisy and fraud, as well as profoundly grieved at seeing the poor people swindled in such an outrageous manner, at once began to denounce Tetzel from the pulpit. But as this failed to have the desired effect, and Tetzel retaliated by denouncing Luther as an arch-heretic, who ought to be burned at the stake, and striving in every possible way to inflame the passions of the ignorant against the honest preacher, Luther determined to write his famous "Theses," containing ninety-five clear and distinct theological propositions, to prove that Papal indulgence, or remission of punishment for sin, was a fraudulent and ungodly thing, and in which he furthermore rebukes and denounces many other abuses and errors of the Roman Church. This celebrated document, in Luther's own handwriting, was publicly posted, by himself, upon the door of the cathedral in Wittenberg, on the thirty-first of October, 1517. To the "Theses" was attached a paper containing a challenge to any one, priest or layman, to debate the questions involved in them publicly, so that the charges preferred by the writer against the clergy and the abuses of the Church, might be ventilated, the truth vindicated, and the spiritual welfare of the people secured. No one accepted the bold challenge. The news of Luther's daring attack upon the doctrine of the Mother Church and the hereditary usages and privileges of the Papal dominion, spread like wild-fire, and the substance of his theological pronunciamento, in the words of an old historian, "flew throughout all Christendom as if the angels themselves were the messengers and bearers thereof." Soon Luther's name was upon every tongue, and his "Theses" the theme of mingled praise and censure.

Thus had Luther, the champion of Christianity, entered the arena, a poor monk, to wrestle with the Pope, the spiritual ruler of the world, the supreme arbiter in the affairs of empires. But he entered the conflict fearlessly, calmly, conscious of Divine assistance, and buoyed by his implicit trust in a final victory.

CHAPTER VI.

MELANCHTHON—THE GATHERING STORM—CARDINAL CAJETAN.

LUTHER, in his efforts to reform the Church, had the assistance of tried and eloquent friends, to whose efforts the cause of truth and religion is deeply indebted. Chief among these illustrious men is to be named Philip Melanchthon, born February 16, 1497, at Bretten, in the Palatinate, now the Grand Duchy, of Baden. The parents of Melanchthon were humble and very pious people, and the fruits of their Christian training were abundantly apparent in the life of their gifted and noble son. Melanchthon distinguished himself by his studious habits and wonderful progress in all the branches of human knowledge while at school, and became a professor in the University of Wittenberg in his twenty-first year. Luther says of him, "Although but a mere boy in appearance, I freely admit that he surpasses me in learning, and I will befriend and defend him as long as I live." Not only did the erudite Melanchthon assist his friend and colaborer, Luther, by means of his profound theological knowledge and powerful pen, but he also exerted a great and salutary influence over the naturally impetuous temper of his illustrious friend, soothing the turbulent emotions of his mighty spirit by means of his own childlike tenderness and cool, persuasive eloquence.

Luther's protest against the abuse of Papal power, and his denouncement of the errors of the Roman Church, permeated the land with surprising rapidity. The pamphlet was distributed in countless numbers, and translated into various languages. This was one of the immediate and noteworthy results of that inestimable blessing of civilization, the art of printing, whose power, though just sprung into life, was already beginning to be felt with marked effect throughout the world. Multitudes, who had become tired of the despotic yoke of a profligate priesthood, and the crushing power of dictatorial Rome, rejoiced at the event, and were loud in their admiration of the frank and courageous denouncer of superstition and wrong. Others, again, dreaded the serious consequences that might follow, and the cruel persecution that would pursue and crush the daring innovator. A simultaneous howl of execration arose from the adherents of the Papacy, and prelates and priests denounced Luther as an infamous heretic. The notorious Tetzel caused Luther's pamphlet to be burned in public, and demanded that its author be thrown into the flames along with his sacrilegious work. Many of the leading priests of the realm, among them prominently the Dominican monk, Sylvester Prierias, violently attacked Luther through the press. Thus, at once, were fierce factions arrayed against each other. Finally, rumors of the difficulty reached Rome. But Luther remained calm and unmoved. To the anxious inquiries of his friends he replied, "If this work has not been begun in the Lord's name, it will soon be destroyed; but if it is begun in his name, and for his glory, let Jehovah reign."

However, it should be well understood that Luther, at this particular time, did not contemplate a general and thorough reformation of the Church. His first object was to remove a glaring blemish, an unscriptural and vicious construction of doctrinal truths, from the records of the Holy Mother Church ; to restore the worship at its altars to its original purity; and, by so doing, to serve its acknowledged Head. Luther sincerely believed that the honor and dignity of the Holy Father had been seriously compromised and violated, by this shameless and wanton traffic in the Pope's "indulgences," in connection with the immoral doctrines preached to the people by those who made it a business to peddle them throughout the realm. He even sent a copy of his tract against this abuse to the Pope, assuring him that great trouble and harm was being done by these creatures, and that such a thing certainly was being effected without the Holy Father's knowledge and permission. But Luther's modest and respectful epistle had but a very sorry reception at the court of infallibility in Rome. It was at once determined to make the audacious rebel against Papal authority to feel the weight of its arm, and the terror of its frown. Pope Julius ordered his arrest and delivery before the Roman ecclesiastical tribunal. But, through the interposition of Luther's excellent sovereign, the Elector of Saxony, it was finally decreed that the investigation of the case should take place in Germany. The Pope ordered Cardinal Cajetan, his embassador to the German Court, and who was then residing in the city of Augsburg, to bring Luther to that place and try him for his offense. Luther was summoned in due form, and, in spite of the advice of many anxious friends, immediately accepted the citation. To his friends he said: "What have I to lose? My house is in order. Nothing remains but my frail body. Should they take that, they will probably deprive me of a few hours of earthly existence, but they can not touch my soul." He performed the journey to within three miles of Augsburg on foot, where, owing to physical suffering, he was compelled to engage a countryman and his wagon to take him to the city, where he arrived on the 7th of October, 1518.

The cardinal, in a note couched in the most urbane and flattering terms, requested Luther to appear before him at once; but, having been warned by friends to be very careful of his person, Luther refused the audience unless protected by an imperial safe-guard, which was at last reluctantly granted. Well was it for Luther that affectionate and shrewd friends watched over him, for the cardinal had been instructed to secure him at all hazards, and to render him harmless for the future, either by imprisonment or death. Thrice did the wily cardinal put the sturdy and conscientious monk upon trial, in order to convict him of error or heresy; or, if possible, to contradict him through the Bible, the only book upon which Luther proposed to base his defense.

The cardinal flatly demanded, at last, that Luther should recant, and cease teaching his obnoxious doctrine, provided he desired to escape imminent and condign punishment. But Luther declared, "I have subordinated my will to the will of my Heavenly Father, and if I had a hundred heads, instead of one, I would rather lose them all than to abjure the doctrines of the true faith."

Only through the strenuous exertions of

friends and the grace of Providence did Luther escape for the present the danger that threatened his liberty, as well as his life.

However, it was not in the programme of his foes to give this liberal-ideaed agitator rest. Only the means used to compass his final destruction were changed. The harsh exercise of ecclesiastical authority was changed to cajolery and inquisitorial cunning.

The Pope determined to confer upon the stanch friend of Luther, Frederick of Saxony, the anointed order of the Golden Rose, and delegated his chamberlain, the astute Carl von Millitz, to be the bearer of the bauble to the Saxon Court. The Pope instructed the embassador to make the formal presentation of the order the occasion for a request from him for the delivery of the person of Luther into the hands of the Roman authorities, or at least to endeavor to effect a change in the opinions of the prince in favor of the Pope's designs. The result of all these machinations was, that Luther, in January, 1519, was compelled to meet the smiling, crafty Roman courtier at the Residence in Altenburg, and, finally, to promise that he would allow the matter to rest for the present, and to cease the publication of his denunciatory tracts against Tetzel and his adherents.

Luther promised this upon condition that his opponents remain silent, and cease, as he expressed it, to "goad him;" but under no pressure or condition whatever could Luther be prevailed upon to recant what he had taught concerning the Gospel. His steadfast reply was, "I have only taught the truth."

But it is evident that Providence had decreed a far different result from that proposed to be encompassed by the priest-power of Rome. The truce entered into at Altenburg by the Pope's embassador and the humble monk Luther, did not suit the vindictive priesthood of the Roman Catholic hierarchy, nor did it for a moment influence them to desist from hurling anathemas upon Luther's teachings, and the vilest sort of slanders upon himself. In this way did they become unwilling instruments, in the hands of an all-wise Providence, for the propagation of the very truths they were endeavoring to crush with such indecent rage.

CHAPTER VII.

LUTHER *vs.* ECK—LUTHER'S EXCOMMUNICATION—HE BURNS THE POPE'S BULL.

DR. ECK, Professor in the University of Ingolstadt, and the most learned of all Luther's opponents, challenged him to a public debate upon all the disputed doctrinal points, the disputation to take place in one of the public halls of Leipzig. Luther could not, nor would, had he been able to do so, evade the challenge. He accepted it forthwith, and met his renowned opponent as agreed. For three weeks, from June the 27th to July 17th, 1519, did this gigantic intellectual struggle continue between the opposing theological champions. The great hall of the

University of Leipzig was daily crowded by multitudes attracted by the novel spectacle, and deeply interested in its consequences. Finally, public acclamation unanimously decided the complete triumph of Luther over the crest-fallen champion of the Papacy, Rev. Dr. Eck.

Chagrined and incensed, Eck immediately hurried to Rome, and succeeded in persuading the Pope to issue a Bull, or proclamation, declaring the contumacious Luther and all who would believe in his heresies, excommunicated; that is, deprived of all communion with the Church, void of honor, subject to the loss of all worldly goods, and deprived of the right to hold office. The effect of the Pope's Bull was not entirely satisfactory to the dominant Church party and the bitter enemies of the Reformer. Eck, who had been the prime instigator of this affair, on his return to Germany, was sometimes obliged to secrete himself or avoid certain localities in order to escape violent public demonstrations of censure upon himself, and in many parts of the country the civil authorities failed to proclaim the Papal decree, or, if posted in the market places, it was torn to pieces by the infuriated populace. At other points, however, such as Lowen, Cologne, and Mayence, the Pope's Bull was received with joy and enthusiasm, and Luther's writings were burned with intense satisfaction in the public squares of those cities.

During all this tumultuous period, Luther himself did not remain idle. He not only refused to acknowledge the validity of the ban, but immediately published a sharp and vigorous rejoinder, under the title, "Concerning Eck's New Bulls and Lies." In this pamphlet Luther demonstrated so clearly and conclusively the wicked intentions of the Pope's edict, and the falsehood of its statements, that many persons who had hitherto held themselves aloof began to see the true merits of the controversy, and sided with the friends of truth and enlightenment. They insisted that it was the duty of the Pope to recall his unwise and distorted Bull, and to punish Eck for his presumptuous interference in the matter. It was argued that unless the Pope would pursue this course without delay, it would prove him recreant to his spiritual duty, the enemy of God, the persecutor of Christ and his Church, and far more dangerous to its interests than the veriest infidel could be. Says a contemporary writer, "Verily, heretofore has our holy faith never been denounced in as hellish and accursed a manner as is done in this blasphemous Bull."

Luther, exasperated by the cruel denunciation of himself and the wholesale destruction of his writings by the priestly faction, determined to prove to the world "how easy it is to burn books;" consequently, he caused proclamation to be made, in due form, to the University of Wittenberg and the townsmen, that, "on the tenth day of December, at the hour of nine o'clock in the morning, the antichristian decrees of the Pope would be destroyed publicly by fire." At the time appointed, the pyre was accordingly erected near the Elster Gate of the town, and in the presence of the professors and students of the University and a large concourse of citizens, Luther solemnly proceeded to throw into the flames the statutes concerning the infallibility of the Pope, the ecclesiastical laws defining the rights and immunities of the Roman Catholic clergy, and the Pope's Bull against himself. He performed the act with the words, "Because thou hast presumed to trouble and harass the servants of the Most High, be thou, therefore, troubled and destroyed by fire everlasting." The writings of some of Luther's chief opponents, such as Eck and Emsa, were also made to feed the flames.

Thus, in the eyes of all liberal-minded men, had just and deserved expression been given to the popular estimate in which the corrupt canonical laws enforced by the Pope and his clergy were held—laws as disgraceful to the Church as they were blasphemous in the sight of Heaven. Some of these canons gave expression to views such as these: "The Pope and his associates are not required to obey, nor are they bound to become subject to, God's commandments;" and, "If the Pope, through his own wickedness, should cause multitudes to fall into the bottomless pit, yet would no one have the right to punish him," etc.

Still, the unprecedented temerity of Luther's revolt against the authority of the Papal throne caused an immense sensation every-where, and the news of his bold action penetrated to every part of the Christian world. As a general thing, Luther's course was applauded, meeting with especial, although secret, favor at the courts of various minor sovereigns, who believed that the time had now come when it would be possible to restrict the unlimited power of the Pope to some natural bounds—a result which neither the diplomacy of courts nor the force of hostile armies in sanguinary battles had heretofore been able to accomplish.

Luther, in a forcible and concisely-written pamphlet, published under the title of "Reasons why the Works of the Pope and his Followers were Burned," gave to the world a full account of that important event, so pregnant with grave results, and which may be said to have irrevocably inaugurated the great work of the Reformation.

CHAPTER VIII.

LUTHER BEFORE THE DIET AT WORMS.

ALTHOUGH, as before stated, Luther had, in the beginning of the controversy, only protested and rebelled against the shameless abuse of the indulgence privilege, and had duly acknowledged the Roman See as the supreme tribunal in all matters pertaining to the Church, yet he did not fail to meet the crisis now forced upon him with the wonted fearlessness and sublime heroism of his nature. He at once determined to free himself and the Church from the foul incubus which for centuries had rested upon and dwarfed its energies, and to crush at one decisive blow the vile and superstitious dogmas inculcated and enforced by a degraded hierarchy. He declared the entire doctrine of Papal indulgence and the remission of sins a swindle of the priesthood, and denounced the Pope himself as an usurper. He denounced monachism and the worship of images; announced himself as opposed to the prevailing system of mass-saying for the repose of the souls of the dead, and declared the enforced celibacy of the clergy unnatural and unscriptural. He also refused to acknowledge the right of the priesthood to deprive communicants of the privilege and benefits of the holy sacrament, and sharply censured many other unbiblical doctrines and ordinances of the Roman Catholic Church.

The Pope formally demanded of the Emperor of Germany, Charles V, the punishment of the audacious "heretic," but the emperor determined to give Luther the benefit of the laws, and ordered his trial to take place before the Imperial Diet, at Worms. In the Spring of the year 1521, Luther was requested to appear before that august body, to defend his cause, and abide by the decision of the German Parliament. The emperor granted him a passport and an escort as far as Worms. Full of faith in the justness of his cause, and assured of Divine protection, Luther left Wittenberg, and prepared to face his influential and numerous enemies. His friends were in great trouble about the proposed journey, and attempted to dissuade him from making the venture, as they feared that a fate similar to that of the lamented Huss, at Constance, one hundred and six years before, might befall him; but Luther replied: "I am called to Worms, and to Worms I will go. Though they build fires between Wittenberg and Worms so high that the flames touch heaven, I will confront them in the name of the Lord, and acknowledge Christ and his Gospel. Huss was burned to ashes, but the truth was not destroyed with him. Christ still lives, despite of all the devices of Hell and the powers of the Prince of Darkness. If there were as many devils in Worms as there are tiles upon its roofs, I would enter the place, face the jaws of the Behemoth, and test the terror of his teeth."

Having received the imperial safe-conduct, through the exertions of his sovereign, the elector, Luther quietly proceeded upon his long journey, and safely arrived at Worms on the sixteenth of April. When Luther entered the city, a great multitude assembled to look upon the stalwart monk who had dared to brave the ire and power of the Pope as neither king nor emperor dared to do. On the following day still greater crowds thronged to see him, on his way to the assembled Diet, where all the grand civil and ecclesiastical dignitaries of the realm, including the emperor himself, a king, six electors, twenty-four dukes, and over two hundred and fifty noblemen were assembled to hear him.

Luther, however, entered the magnificent and crowded halls with calm, dignified, and resolute bearing, unabashed by the splendor of the scene or the novelty of his situation.

He was asked whether he acknowledged the authorship of certain published works, the titles of which were read to him by an official of the Diet. He replied in the affirmative; but when he was formally asked whether he was ready to recant the doctrines he had taught in these writings, he requested that the Diet grant him twenty-four hours respite to meditate upon a subject of such deep importance to the soul and its salvation, and to prepare a suitable answer. The delay was granted. Luther passed the whole of the succeeding night in fervent prayer and profound meditation. On the following day, as he was about to enter the Diet, an old veteran, named George von Frundsberg, approached him, and tapping Luther upon the shoulder in a friendly way, said: "My honest little monk, thou art about to enter upon a path of danger the like of which neither I nor any other old soldier has ever trodden, even in the hottest rage of battle. However, if thou art right, and assured of the truth of thy cause, go forward, in God's name, and fear not. The Lord will never forsake thee!" Many others, princes and noblemen, encouraged him with kindly speech, and bade him be of good cheer. Supported by Divine grace, Luther met the crisis like the Christian hero that he was, nor flinched in the least during the trying scene. In a long address, he stated his reasons for pursuing the course he did, and declared his inability conscientiously to abjure the doctrines he had avowed, preached, and defended. On the final demand of the Diet that he should render a short and decisive answer to the question concerning a formal recantation, Luther replied: "Whereas, your Imperial Majesty and illustrious princes require of me an artless and direct answer to your interrogatory, I shall give one that can in no wise be misunderstood; namely, unless that I am subdued by the evidence of Holy Writ, or by clear, intelligent, and undisguised reasons, I can not and *will not* recant. It is neither safe nor desirable to violate conscience. On this I stand; I can not do otherwise. God help me! Amen!"

Profound was the impression which this noble and ever-memorable declaration made upon all present. It thrilled the hearts of Luther's adherents like the clang of the trumpets of victory, and prince and peasant alike were forced to acknowledge the sublime courage of the humble monk, and pay homage to the potency of his chivalric spirit.

His clerical enemies, and the partisans of the Papal corruption in general, however, waxed only the more violent and desperate in proportion to Luther's success. They urged the emperor to withdraw the imperial "Geleitbrief," or safe-guard, from Luther, which permitted him to travel unharmed to and from

Wittenberg, excusing this piece of knavery upon the ground that it was not required of any one to keep promises made to a "heretic." The emperor, however, replied, magnanimously, "Though all the world be full of knaves and treachery, a German emperor will never break his plighted word." Thus, relying upon the protection which his passport afforded him, and which had been extended to embrace a period of twenty days, Luther departed from Worms on his return journey to Wittenberg. Nevertheless, Luther had, in the mean time, been declared an outlaw and arch-heretic by the Papal authorities; that is every body throughout the empire was authorized and commanded to inflict upon him and his kindred all possible harm and violence, even to the taking of life. But the words of the inspired Psalmist, "In the time of trouble he shall hide me in his pavilion; in the secret of his tabernacle shall he hide me; he shall set me on a rock," were never more beautifully or literally exemplified than in the case of Luther. He found a "pavilion," the Lord's "tabernacle," in the mountain fortress Wartburg.

CHAPTER IX.

LUTHER WAYLAID BY HIS FRIENDS—THE WARTBURG ASYLUM.

ON the morning of April 26, 1521, Luther left Worms for Wittenberg, in the company of a few friends. Near Oppenheim, he was overtaken by the emperor's herald, Sturm, who acted as escort as far as Friedberg. At this place, the imperial herald was sent back to Worms as the bearer of dispatches, but which was simply a ruse on the part of Luther's friends to rid themselves of his presence. His place was taken by a young knight, belonging to the suite of the Landgrave Philip of Hessia, who had become an enthusiastic adherent of the

Lutheran doctrines. All the arrangements for the personal safety of Luther had been secretly perfected by his noble friend and sovereign, Frederick the Wise, with the efficient assistance of the prince's private secretary, Spalatin, a learned Doctor of Divinity and admirer of the Reformer. It had been determined by Luther's friends, that he and his party should be attacked upon the highway, at some eligible point near Castle Wartburg, by an armed force of masked horsemen, dragged with great apparent violence upon a horse held ready for the purpose, and hurried off by the kidnapping party into the mountains, safe from pursuit or detection. Though Luther was aware that powerful friends were engaged in attempts to preserve his life against the murderous designs of his enemies, he was entirely ignorant of the friendly plot to abduct him, and of the means made ready to accomplish it. The utmost secrecy was essential, in order to thwart the spies of the priesthood, and prevent the

Papal authorities from knowing the true state of affairs. The object was to make Luther's enemies, and the human bloodhounds upon his track, believe that he had been attacked and murdered by a band of fanatics, in pursuance of the Pope's ban of outlawry.

All along the route, from Worms as far as Eisenach, Luther was received at prominent points with enthusiastic expressions of reverence and love. Many noblemen, and even some of the most distinguished of the clergy, vied with each other in demonstrations of esteem and admiration for the sturdy opponent of ecclesiastical despotism, and the fearless champion of Gospel truth. At Harsfeld, for instance, a brilliant procession of nobles and citizens of the town, headed by the Abbot of Harsfeld Abbey, met Luther, and escorted him into town, where he and his party were treated to a public dinner in the Abbey refectory. Here, and in defiance of the emperor's decree ordering him to abstain from public preaching, Luther delivered a soul-stirring sermon, at the earnest solicitation of the resident clergy and the multitude. At Eisenach similar public demonstrations awaited him, and his entry into the gates of his "dear town," as Luther loves to call Eisenach, resembled the triumphal entry of a prince.

On the following day, while Luther and a few of his friends were quietly pursuing their way toward Wittenberg, and while passing through a narrow defile in the mountains in the neighborhood of the chapel at Glisbach, the denouement of the kidnapping plot followed. A party of mail-clad horsemen, emerging from the adjacent woods, rushed down upon them at a full charge. Luther's brother Jacob, who was in the vehicle with his illustrious brother, jumped out, and escaped in the bushes near the roadside. Dashing up, one of the riders demanded if any of the travelers was named Luther; the latter, rising in response, had a cross-bow placed against his breast, and was ordered to surrender immediately. Two of his companions, terribly frightened, begged for mercy; but Luther, comprehending the plot at a glance, whispered to them, in Latin, "*Confidi, amici nostri sunt*—fear not, they are our friends"—and quietly gave himself up. Luther was stripped of his priestly robes, a horseman's cloak was thrown over his shoulders, and he was bound upon a horse held ready for the purpose. His astonished friends were ordered to proceed on their way, and the troop, with their prisoner, dashed into the forest skirting the road.

The news of the arrest and abduction of Luther spread every-where, and the plot was so successfully and secretly accomplished, that Luther's enemies, and many of his friends, actually believed him to have been incarcerated for life in some gloomy dungeon of the inquisition, or killed by the dagger of some fanatical Papist.

Luther arrived safely, at midnight, at the

Wartburg, a strong mountain fortress overlooking the town of Eisenach, in Saxony, where every preparation had been made by the Elector Frederick for his friend's safety and comfort.

Luther felt grateful for the care shown by his friends for his personal safety, and attempted to adapt himself to his novel circumstances; but it was an irksome task for a free and aspiring spirit like his to be circumscribed by the narrow limits of a feudal castle. The eagle loves to sun his wings in the limitless empyrean, unfettered, sovereign, sublime; cage him, and his royal spirit becomes broken, and though his prison bars are made of solid gold, he frets his pinions angrily against them, and sighs for his ancient freedom. Thus it was with the captive Luther.

Luther's personal appearance at this time was very different from what it was at a later period in his life, and as we behold him in the famous picture by Cranach, when he had become fleshy and comfortably stout. Up to the time of his involuntary residence at the Wartburg, he had not improved physically since the time of his celebrated colloquium with Dr. Eck, at Leipzig, where, naturally of medium size only, he appeared so excessively lean, by reason of severe study, that "one could count the bones of his body through the skin," as he himself humorously remarked. Nor had the succeeding years of anxiety and labor contributed to lesson this defect. The governor of the castle treated Luther with extreme respect and kindness. He was known to his attendants by the name of "Esquire Georg," and allowed brief excursions on horseback to points of interest adjacent to the castle. In these excursions, he was always followed by a trusty servant, and disguised in the garb of a common country squire. Now and then he was allowed to communicate with some of his relatives and most intimate friends, but many of his letters were destroyed by the commandant of the Wartburg, who feared that some of the missives might fall into the hands of spies, and betray the residence of his illustrious guest. In many of his letters he speaks of the Wartburg in metaphor, and it seems that he loved to call it his "island of Patmos," judging from the frequency with which this title appears in his Wartburg epistles.

His restless mind found ample and congenial work in his seclusion in all kinds of polemics. He devoted himself to the refutation of great numbers of pamphlets published by his opponents against himself, and was indefatigable in his exposure of the frauds of priestcraft, and his attacks upon the gross abuses in the Roman Church. His new doctrines were assailed on every side by vigorous writers; nor were his assailants in the least particular as to the means they used to blacken his character and destroy his cause. But through it all, the heart of Luther never descended to chicane or personal malice, and in every thing that emanated from his keen and facile pen brightly shines the light of a pure and noble spirit.

In spite of every precaution, Luther's place of concealment was discovered, and when the governor of the Wartburg announced the disagreeable news to him, he at once declared his willingness to seek some other asylum, or face his enemies directly. At last it was decided to attempt another ruse upon the enemy. Luther wrote a long letter to Spalatin, dated from some imaginary and distant point of the empire, and the letter was allowed to fall, as if by mere accident, into the hands of his persecutors. The plan succeeded; and, though, the efforts of the Papists were not abated, they were placed upon a false trail.

His irksome confinement, however, and intense application to literary work, preyed upon his system, and begun to cloud his sunny mind with a haze of strange hallucinations.

While in this condition, the well-known anecdote is related of him, that while engaged at midnight in his apartment, on some important work, Satan appeared in person to torment him, and that Luther rid himself of this fiery and unwelcome guest by hurling his huge inkstand at the intruder's head.

His heart was filled with an uncontrollable yearning for his dear Wittenberg; so, some time during November, he left the Wartburg secretly, made his way to Wittenberg, and remained there several days, secreted in the house of his friend Arnsdorf, where he met and consulted with many of his adherents. Reaching his mountain asylum again in safety, cheered and refreshed, he began his great work of translating the Bible, beginning with the New Testament, as he could not attempt the translation of the Old without its assistance, as he states in a letter to Arnsdorf. His translation of the Bible created a profound sensation in the public mind. This is apparent in the statement of one of Luther's contemporaries, Erasmus Aeber, who says: "Doctor Martinus is a veritable German Cicero. He hath not only shown us what true religion is, but hath also reformed the German language. No living writer on earth can be compared to him." Our astonishment increases when we remember that the translation of the New Testament was completed in the period of scarcely two months, notwithstanding frequent interruptions and much anxiety caused by the indiscreet actions of some of his noisy followers. Luther's translation of the Old Testament followed soon after, and in 1534 the immortal work upon which he had labored so faithfully within the gloomy walls of the Wartburg was finished, and the first complete German Bible given to the world.

It was a matter of astonishment to Europe that Luther, amid all his travels and active labors, could present so very perfect a translation of the whole Bible. But a single word explains it all. He had a rigid system of doing something every day. In answer to a question how he did it, Luther said, "Nulla dies sine versu—not a day without a verse." It was this persistence and energy that brought him soon to the close of his Bible.

CHAPTER X.

LUTHER LEAVES THE WARTBURG—FALSE PROPHETS.

N the third day of March, 1522, in spite of the earnest protest of his friend, the elector, Luther left the Wartburg, disguised in his knightly costume, and reached Wittenberg in safety, where disturbances had taken place which seemed to threaten with destruction the entire work of the Reformation which Luther, so far, had succeeded in accomplishing.

A few rebellious spirits, namely, had arrived in Wittenberg, who claimed to be acting under special Divine inspiration, and demanded the regeneration of the Church by force of arms.

These persons had been joined by Dr. Karlstadt, a colaborer of Luther's, and professor in the University. These men, haranguing the people, incited a riot, which culminated in a general assault upon the churches of the place, the destruction of pictures of saints, the paraphernalia of Romish ritualism, and other iconoclastic proceedings.

As soon as Luther heard of these deplorable outrages, he determined to use all of his personal influence and authority to repress the demon of riot and revolution. He quit the Wartburg on horseback, and during the shelter of a dark night. It was the third day of March, 1522. Heedless of all personal danger, oblivious to the dread ban of the Church resting upon his head, and the fact that, as an outlaw, his life was in the hands of any lurking assassin, he hurried on to Wittenberg, arriving there in safety. To his sovereign, who had so strenuously remonstrated with him against the apparent folly of the act, he wrote:

LUTHER LEAVING THE WARTBURG.

"I go to Wittenberg protected by a far higher and stronger power than that of my sovereign; nor do I desire the protection of your Royal Highness. Yea; I hold that I am protecting you rather than that you are protecting me. This matter shall not and can not be helped or mended by the sword. The Lord alone must labor here, without the aid of human hands. He, therefore, that hath the greatest faith will command the greatest means of protection." And so it proved to be. Luther's earnest and potential words, like oil poured upon the troubled waters, soothed the angry waves of religious excitement, and again brought peace within the walls of his beloved Wittenberg.

Unfortunately, however, for the general peace and safety of the people, the spirit of rebellion and sedition began to show itself all over Germany, and broke out in fearful violence in many places. Thomas Muenzer, Dean of Allstadt, in Thuringia, declared that he was the Holy Ghost, and preached that it was not only necessary that all men should be relieved of the yoke and despotism of Papal dominion, but that all the authority of civil government must be abolished, because every Christian was a free man, and exempt from all tribute to the authorities, or obedience to the laws. Such doctrine was very suggestive and agreeable to an enslaved and oppressed peasantry, groaning under the lash of priests, and impoverished by an extravagant and debauched nobility. Inflamed and goaded by the harangues of crazy or designing demagogues, the German peasants, in great and armed crowds, swept from place to place, burning, pillaging, and destroying every thing in their path, and leveling the monuments of feudal power and the strongholds of mighty lords with the dust.

Luther was kept busy in efforts to allay the raging social and political storm by means of mouth and pen. He wrote numerous important pamphlets, addressed to the people, to show the madness and criminality of these proceedings, and expounding the Scriptural injunctions concerning the duty of all men to subject themselves to magistrates and ordained authorities. But even the powerful hand and mind of Luther was inadequate to allay the tempest, and bid the wild waves of rebellion cease from their horrid work of destruction. Kings and nobles banded together to preserve their existence, and in the name of the law threw their disciplined cohorts upon the demoralized and illy-armed peasant mobs. Many thousands of these were massacred in battle, and the ring-leader, Muenzer, and a number of his most prominent assistants were captured and beheaded. These deplorable occurrences took place during the year 1525, an eventful one in the annals of the German Fatherland.

In the same year an important event occurred in the life of the great Reformer; namely, his marriage to Catherine von Bora;

a step whose blessed and permanent influence upon himself and the cause he championed can not be estimated.

CHAPTER XI.

LUTHER AS HUSBAND, FATHER, AND FRIEND.

IN most of the biographies of the great Reformer, we contemplate him as the stern and wrathful assailant of the abuses of the Divine Word, as the bold and fearless defender of his dogmas, as the rough and ever-ready champion of Christ's Church, a valiant warrior of the Cross, armed *cap-a-pie* in defense of the right. We hear but little of Luther as the affectionate husband, the loving father, the devoted friend, the cheerful lover of music and of the beauties of nature; nor do we hear enough of his universal benevolence—every-where drying the tears of affliction as far as his stalwart arms could reach —and yet what wealth of love and tenderness, of manliness combined with the sweetest and most child-like simplicity, do we find in this truly loyal and honest German nature! At work or resting in the home circle, at the altar or in the chamber of the sick and dying, praying or playing, in the midst of old or young, the rich and noble or the poor and unlettered, we find the same great and noble spirit, the same unalterable fidelity to truth and the God of truth. His love of children in itself is one of the loveliest idyls, pervaded with pure and tranquil joy, yet full of the stronger traits of character; for Luther ever strove to educate his children to shun hypocrisy in every shape, training them by precept and example to be strong and noble men and true-hearted women. These are the softer outlines of that granite Rock of the Reformation, against which the surly tides of darkness and priestly hate beat in vain; who fearlessly faced the thunders of the Vatican and the terrors of imperial bans;

the banner-bearer of the host that fought for spiritual freedom; the man who knew and cared only for the honor of God and the welfare of his native land. Lessing says: "I venerate Luther to such a degree that I am glad to have discovered some faults in him, otherwise I would have been in danger of apotheosizing him. The traces of the human which I find upon him are as precious to me as the most dazzling of his perfections."

When Luther had firmly laid the foundation of a new Church, he decided upon removing the last remnant of Popish folly with which the freedom of his actions was still hampered—he determined to transform the cold, celibate monk into the ardent and affectionate husband and father; the dreary cell into a home of quiet joys and domestic happiness. Long ago he had demonstrated that priestly vows of celibacy were contrary to the teachings of Christ, and in direct conflict with the whole tenor and spirit of Christianity. For the clergy of the new Church the holy institution of matrimony had become a duty as well as a moral necessity, and yet Luther had himself hesitated to take the final and irrevocable step. To the request of his friends that he should place the sacred seal of the Church upon the bonds of matrimony by his individual action, he returned an evasive answer; he wished some clergyman of higher rank than himself to take the solemn initiatory step, and for this end he had fixed his eyes upon the Elector Archbishop of Mentz. To this august personage he wrote in his usual bold style: "I can not see how a man can remain in a condition of celibacy without incurring the displeasure and wrath of God; and, surely, it must be dreadful should he be thus found when death approaches; for what can he answer when the Creator shall say, 'I created thee a man, whom I desired not to be alone— where is thy wife?'" At a later period he wrote, probably after the archbishop had declined the request of Luther, "If my own marriage would be the means of strengthening your purpose and determining your action, I shall not hesitate in preceding your Royal Highness in this matter."

Luther remained true to his resolve. Catherine von Bora, a former nun, became his wife — a noble, high-spirited, and devoted woman, in every way worthy to be the companion and counselor of such a man.

The step he had reluctantly yet in the spirit of duty taken, proved to be a most fortunate one to himself, and of great importance to the holy cause in which Luther was then so profoundly engaged; for it had, in consequence, gained a calm and secluded family asylum, where its exalted friends and champions could assemble and rest from the toils of their perilous warfare; where they could gather renewed strength for coming trials in the wholesome atmosphere of love and piety; in a home around whose fireside the influence of a loving woman was ever found brightening the furrowed brows of care-worn man, cheering the faint-hearted, and inspiring the mighty spirits there engaged in molding the destiny of nations.

Luther's friends visited frequently at his house; none more so than Melanchthon, who delighted to hear Luther sing and play when surrounded by his children. Luther used to call such occasions his "Home Cantorium;" and it is well known how dearly Luther loved music, and how devotedly he worshiped at its golden shrine during his hours of leisure, at school, in the university, and even in the dreary cloister cell.

Luther was not only a poet, to whom we owe some of the most majestic hymns ever written, but a composer of much merit, having composed the music which accompanies many of his grandest songs. His familiar hymns are characterized by truth, soul-stirring power, and profound pathos, and his melodies, though simple, are in harmony with the lofty words. This is beautifully exemplified in the hymn, "Eine feste Burg ist unser Gott," the stirring battle-anthem of the Reformation, which, with its triumphant peals, led the indomitable hosts of Protestantism to final victory.

D'Aubigne, in his "History of the Reformation," gives the following anecdote concerning the effects of music upon Luther. The incident took place during his residence in the Augustinian monastery, at Wittenberg: "One day, overcome with sadness, he shut himself in his cell, and for several days and nights suffered no one to approach him. One of his friends, Lukas Edemberger, uneasy about him, took with him some young boys, choral singers, and went and knocked at the door of his cell. No one opened or answered. Edemberger broke open the door, and found Luther stretched on the floor without any sign of life. His friend tried in vain to recall his senses. Then the young choristers began to sing a sweet hymn. Their clear voices acted like a charm on the poor monk, to whom music had always been a source of delight, and by degrees his consciousness returned."

Luther, in one of his letters, says: "I am not satisfied with him who professeth to scorn the art of music; because I deem music to be not a human but a Divine gift. It maketh the heart glad, and putteth Satan to flight. Next to theology, I give the highest rank and the greatest honor to music."

From motives such as these, he diligently cultivated the art of music in his family. After the day's weary labors were over; after having preached from the pulpit, or taught in the lecture-room to the gathered youth of the land, who listened to his teachings with reverential affection; after important consultations with his brethren in the faith, or a decision upon some weighty point of action with his colaborers and comrades in the holy cause; or after having labored all day with the pen, throwing off addresses and pamphlets to the people, a matter which he considered of far greater importance than the most learned and brilliant theological disputations,—no matter how the day had passed, the evening was invariably devoted to the enjoyments of the domestic circle. Lively conversation, jokes and sparkling repartee, singing and music upon various instruments were then in order, Luther himself accompanying the songs upon a guitar or with the flute, of which he was a master. A sweet, wholesome spirit of piety pervaded the whole house, and it can be truly said that a happier home than that of Luther never existed on earth.

CHAPTER XII.

A CHARACTERISTIC LETTER—HIS WIFE AND CHILDREN.

WE can give no better glimpse into the depths of Luther's loving heart than that which is afforded by the perusal of a letter to his eldest son, John, or his "little Hanschen," as he loved to call him, written while Luther was at Castle Coburg. At that time the Imperial Diet was in session at Augsburg, but Luther could not attend it, because the ban of the Empire was still in force against him. However, in order to be as near as possible to the Diet, he took up his abode at Coburg. Under the heavy weight of serious and rapidly accumulating labor in the interests of the struggling Church, he never forgot the tender ties that bound him to the loved ones at home; and the following quaint epistle to his "four-year-old" will interest the reader in this connection:

"My Darling Little Son,—It pleases me to learn that thou art studying so well and so diligently. Continue in doing this, my child, and when I return home I will bring thee some beautiful presents. I know an exceedingly pretty garden, wherein very many children do enjoy and disport themselves. They are clad in golden garments, and gather beautiful apples under the trees; they sing, gambol, and are merry, having also pretty little ponies, with golden reins and saddles of silver. Thereupon I inquired of the Master that owneth the garden whose children these were. He answered, 'These are the children who love to pray and study, and are pious.' Whereupon I replied, 'Dear Sir, I, too, have a little son, named Johnny Luther; may he not also come into the garden, so that he can eat beautiful apples and pears, and ride upon such handsome ponies, and play with these children?' Thereupon the man replied, 'If he loves to pray and learn his lessons, and is pious, he, too, may come into the garden, also Lippus and Jost, his playmates; and when they all shall come together, they shall play on fifes and drums and lutes, and all kinds of stringed instruments, and they will dance, and shoot with tiny cross-bows.' And the man showed me into a fine green in the garden, arranged for dancing, and around it were displayed beautiful golden fifes, drums, and fine silver cross-bows. But it was still early in the day, and the children had not yet eaten their meal; therefore I could not wait to see the dancing, and said to the man, "O, dear Sir, I will hasten unto him, and tell him to be sure to pray diligently, to be pious, and to study with ardor, so that he, too, may come into this beautiful garden.' Whereupon the man said, 'Be it so; go and write him thus.'

"Therefore, my dear Johnny, study and pray dutifully, and inform Lippus and Jost, also, that they study and pray, so that you may come together to the Garden. May the Omnipotent Father in heaven watch over thee! Give love to Cousin Lena, and a kiss for my sake.

"Thy loving father,
"MARTIN LUTHER.
"Anno 1530."

Only from the deep fountain of a pure and loving heart could such an epistle emanate. It is a grand and mighty, yet humble and childlike, spirit, that portrays in these quaint lines the fervor of paternal affection, and opens to our view that sacred temple of his soul where the shrine of his domestic happiness was erected; where the "angels of the household," his dear wife and beloved children, reigned supreme, endowing his heart with a richness of felicity rarely equaled, and never excelled, in the annals of human entities.

The "Frau Doctor," or "Master Katie," as he was wont to call his darling wife in his humorous letters, in addition to his "Hanschen," blessed him with five other children: Elizabeth, who died shortly after her birth, Magdalene, Martin, Paul, and Margaret.

How delightful it is to get an occasional glimpse of Luther's home-life! and how beautifully did the hope, expressed in his prayer upon his nuptial-day, ripen into blessed fruition: "Dear, heavenly Father! Because thou hast placed me in a station of honor for thy name's sake, and as thou willest me to be called and honored as a parent, grant me thy grace and blessing, that I may devoutly, and in a godly manner, rule and support my dear wife, my children, and servants."

Years after this, and when in the meridian of his life, he remarked, "My Katie is dutiful and kind in all things, more so than I had dared to hope, and I, therefore, account myself richer than Crœsus."

The garden attached to the old homestead was a great source of the purest enjoyment to the family during the Summer, and so was the old-fashioned "Christmas-tree," in the dreary days of dark December. Luther was an ardent lover of nature, worshiping her ever-varying aspects with reverent heart, and gazing upon her charms with the enraptured eye of a Christian poet—feelings which he sought to cultivate in the breasts of his children, and which he never failed to inspire in his friends. Happy were the hours passed in the arbors and flowery paths of his little garden by Luther, surrounded by his family and intimate friends. All present shared in the merriment of the little ones, or lent willing aid in instructing their minds when tired of play. The works of nature were unfolded to them in fables and instructive stories; they were made familiar with science and philosophy; and even Art, with her wonderful picture-map, deigned to give her bright presence to the charmed circle, in the person of Lukas Cranach.

To Luther, children were the golden links of that chain which unites the human and the Divine, the visible to the invisible, the lowest to the highest; and his unquenchable love for nature he once expressed by comparing the Scriptures to a beautiful forest, quaintly saying, "There is not a tree in it but what I have touched with a loving hand."

CHAPTER XIII.

CHRISTMAS IN LUTHER'S HOME—DEATH OF MAGDALENA

IN the sweet home-life of Luther, the Christmas-tree was always a hallowed center of attraction, and his children again occupy the most conspicuous place. Strange, indeed, would it have been had it been otherwise, for he never spoke of his children else than "God's brightest blessings." A celebrated German artist has given to the world a happy representation of one of these tender home-scenes, and many thousand copies of this gem of pictorial art adorn the walls of German households. The picture shows Luther sitting near a Christmas-tree, holding upon his lap his youngest daughter, and by his side sits his faithful wife, clasping his hand in her own. Little Paul is showing him his new hobby-horse; and trumpets, wooden horsemen, apples, and toys of every description in ludicrous chaos encumber the floor. Luther's dearest friend, Melanchthon, is engaged with "little Johnny;" and there, in verity, is to be seen the "beautiful garden," groups of merry-faced children, apples, pears, pretty little ponies with golden reins and silver saddles, also fifes, drums, and silver cross-bows, exactly as was promised in father's letter from Coburg! Johnny is engaged in shooting at the golden fruit hanging amid the branches of the gorgeous fir, and behind the table Cousin Lena is enjoying, with little Martin, the contents of a new picture-book, while in front of them sits Magdalena, close to her doll-wagon, holding in her hands the Christmas angel, which has been taken down from the top of the tree for her especial gratification. A blissful smile irradiates her lovely features as she contemplates her treasures. Happy child! soon herself to be a crowned angel of heaven.

While viewing this superb picture of tranquillity and love, it brings vividly to mind again another instance of that grand heroism of spirit and exalted human love so characteristic of Luther; a scene of mournful yet sublime beauty, touching his lofty, rugged nature with a softness like that which settles around the rough crags of some Alpine peak when the glory of a Summer twilight reaches the world.

Growing steadily in beauty of soul, as well as in graces of body, Magdalena, his beloved daughter, the happy child we see in the picture with the Christmas angel in her embrace, had reached the age of thirteen, when, prostrated by a fatal disease, she lay awaiting the approach of death. The Destroyer has laid his relentless hand upon her; moaning, she battles with increasing agony, while by her bedside, upon his knees, Luther wrestles in prayer over his dying child. Tears are falling heavily over his bronzed cheeks; his heart, torn by pain and love, pleads to Heaven for release from her sufferings. "I love her so dearly!" he exclaims; "but, my Father in heaven, if it is thy will, gladly will I resign her to live with thee forever."

He bends over the child, stroking her pallid cheeks, and softly asks:

"My darling, my daughter! wouldst thou love to remain here with thy father, or wouldst thou rather go home to thy Father in heaven?"

"Dear father," the child replies, twining her white, feeble arms about his neck, "as God wills."

Another flood of tears gushes from the father's eyes at this reply; but he turns his face away so that the child may not perceive his emotion, and tenderly whispers:

"O Father! thou knowest how great is the love I have for her; but yet, living or dying, we are thine."

At last the hour of mortal dissolution arrives. Luther's wife, his "beloved Katie," sat, with tear-stained face, in an obscure corner of the death-chamber, her eyes covered by her hands, unable to witness the agonizing scene. Luther had again knelt by the bedside of his dying daughter, praying God to release his child from her mortal struggles. Then he arose, folded her in his arms, and, laying her burning cheek against his own, he endeavored to soothe her last pangs, although his own heart was nearly broken.

In this manner the spirit of Magdalena forsook its earthly tenement, and soared to heaven. Her last look rested upon the face of her father.

Two days after, the corpse, covered with evergreens and flowers, lay in its coffin, in a darkened chamber in the basement of the house. When the persons who were to carry the coffin had arrived, and with them the friends of the family, full of sorrow and affectionate sympathy, Luther took the hand of one of them, and, in his usual sweet and dignified manner, said:

"We should not grieve thus, dear friends, for I have sent a saint to heaven. O, would that all of us could die as she hath done!"

For the last time, alone and in silence, Luther visited the chamber in which his daughter was sleeping the dreamless sleep of death. He approached the wreathed bier, removed the coffin-lid, and cast a last, lingering look upon the face of his darling, from whose white lips never more would issue the tender words, "My dear, dear father!" Who can express the agony that convulsed the heart of the doting and stricken father! But he only sighed, "My own dear Magdalena, how well it is with thee!" He kissed the cold lips, bowed his head, and supplicated God for strength and solace in this dark hour of inexpressible grief. Calmly he arose, and, turning, closed the little house of his darling child forever.

When Luther again appeared in the midst of his family, he comforted them and said, "It is well with my child, both in soul and body." To his sobbing wife he soothingly said, "It is strange to know that she is now happy and in peace, and that we, nevertheless, are so full of sorrow."

He thereupon calmly gave the necessary orders to the coffin-bearers, and, following them, beheld the corpse of his boloved child placed under the fragrant turf of the church-yard.

CHAPTER XIV.

LUTHER'S CATECHISM—THE DIET AT SPIRE, IN 1529—RESULTS.

IN the year 1528, Luther, by command of the elector, again traveled all over the country, in order to ascertain the condition of the Churches and schools. Everywhere he found the most shameful neglect and sordid ignorance, both among the clergy and the laity. In his capacity as inspector, Luther did all in his power to mitigate this evil, and, as one of the most efficient means for reform, he wrote, in 1529, his well-known Catechism, the same which is still in use in every Protestant school in Germany. He first wrote the small Catechism for the use of families, and then another, called the Great Catechism, for the use of the clergy and public schools. Clear, concise, and most happily adapted to impart religious instruction to youth, no work of a similar character since has been able to supersede Luther's Catechism in the schools and families of Protestant Germany.

In 1529, the Emperor of Germany convened another Diet, in Spire, similar to the one of 1526. On this occasion, the adherents of Papacy were very anxious that no changes should be allowed to be effected in Church government, and that its spiritual as well as material existence should remain *in statu quo*. But the dissenting princes and communal authorities, through their representatives, had prepared a series of resolutions protesting against this action of the Roman hierarchy, which resolutions, with due pomp and solemnity, they presented to Charles V, on the nineteenth day of April, ever memorable in the annals of Christianity, as by this "protest" the word "*Prot-*

estant" obtained its ecclesiastical significance. This protest was again renewed by the dissenters during the Diet held in Augsburg, in 1530, where, on the twenty-fifth day of July, in the presence of the emperor and the assembled dignitaries of the realm, they published and presented their Confession of Faith, drawn up by Melanchthon, and which is generally known as the Augsburg Confession of Faith.

This was a most solemn and imposing event, and while Doctor Bayer was reading the document, the most impressive silence reigned throughout the vast and magnificent hall.

The memorial recapitulated the chief errors and abuses of the Papal Church, and solemnly denounced them; and all the leading theses of the true Christian faith were clearly and incontrovertibly expounded in accordance with the Holy Scriptures. It stated that man, from the very moment of his birth, was full of evil spiritual tendencies and carnal lusts, ignorant of Divine love and mercy, and at war with God, hence in a condition of eternal condemnation; but that Christ, the veritable God-man, had redeemed the world from sin through the divine efficiency of his blood; also, that man can not obtain remission of his sins by his own works, but can only obtain justification before God through the grace and intercession of Christ Jesus, the Lamb of God.

Thus, basing their Confession upon the doctrines of Holy Writ, affirming the tenets of a true Church, and casting from them the errors, abuses, and corruptions of the age, the Protestant princes and representatives of free cities of the Empire declared their reasons for demanding a reform of the Church, and resolutely and unanimously published their determination to free themselves from the guilt and venality of the Roman Catholic Church government.

However, in the same ratio in which the resistance of enlightened Protestantism to Papal oppression developed itself, did the wrath of the priesthood, under the control of the Roman Junto and its adherents, increase in violence, until a murderous war of extermination was imminent. Therefore, in self-defense, the Protestants were forced to enter into the form of a Confederation to defend the new faith at the point of the sword, if necessary. Luther was at first opposed to entering into a compact looking to armed resistance, believing that an abiding faith in the power and assistance of God was all-sufficient, but he finally gave his assent to the arrangement.

The final union and concentration of Protestant power was consummated in 1531, at Schmalkalden, and hence has been called the Schmalkaldian Confederation. By this means the new Protestant power achieved, in 1532, the so-called Treaty of Nuremberg, by which the "heretics" were temporarily guaranteed the free and undisturbed exercise of their religious faith.

CHAPTER XV.

YEARS OF TRIAL AND AFFLICTION—LETTERS—HYMNS.

DURING his life, Luther had to undergo many trials and tribulations; but his stout heart never faltered, nor was his bright and mighty spirit ever weakened or darkened by adversity. Doubtless, an all-wise Providence thus tested his sturdy soul in order that he might prove to coming ages an illustrious prototype of Christian submission to the Divine will, thereby encouraging the faint-hearted, and elucidating by his own bright example the truth and purity of the Holy Scriptures, as well as exemplifying the new life infused into the Apostolic Church through his instrumentality and the grace of Jehovah.

In all his trials and afflictions, the same kind and heavenly Father whose love and mercy he so ably expounded, never allowed Luther to feel the shadow of a doubt concerning the efficacy of prayer, or failed to sustain him with the power of his omnipotent hand. To the fullest extent did the Reformer realize the depth and meaning of the Divine promise: "When thou passest through the waters, I will be with thee; and through the rivers, they shall not overflow thee: when thou walkest through the fire, thou shalt not be burned; neither shall the flame kindle upon thee. For I am the Lord thy God, the Holy One of Israel, thy Savior." (Isaiah xliii, 2, 3.)

In a letter to Duke George of Saxony, Luther says: "I consider my prayer far mightier than all the power and majesty of Satan and his court; if it were not so, Luther would have been destroyed long ago."

The year 1527 was in particular a period of sorrow and suffering for Luther. On the ninth of July, of that year, he was overcome by a disease whose painfulness was such that he compares his sufferings to the affliction of St. Paul. While it lasted he showed the greatest fortitude and Christian resignation, and repeatedly declared his willingness to resign the world, and meet his Creator. Yet, through all, he declared humbly, but firmly: "I say it with a clear conscience, that I have taught the Word of God truthfully, and in the way the Lord appointed me to do. Yea, I affirm that I taught wholesomely and righteously of faith, love, the cross, the sacraments, and other articles of Christian belief. There are those who accuse me of being too severe and violent when I write against Papists and blasphemers of holy things, and endeavor to punish their ungodly acts, false doctrines, and hypocrisy. True, I have been at times exasperated, and have handled my opponents roughly, but never so that it hath repented me. Gentle or harsh, I never desired to harm any one, much less to compass the destruction of his soul; on the contrary, I have ever endeavored that good and salvation should come to all, even my worst enemies." To his wife and children he said: "I commend you unto my dear and faithful Father in heaven. Ye have no worldly goods; however, the Lord, who is the father of the orphan and the refuge of the widow, will sustain you and watch over you." Another sore trial, in addition, came upon him in the course of this year. A pestilence broke out in Wittenberg, and Luther's house, among many others, was converted into an asylum for the sick and dying. His life and that of his dear ones was daily exposed to the greatest peril; yet he never left the place, acquitting himself most devotedly of his sacred duties as a minister of the Gospel, notwithstanding the urgent request of the elector that he and his family should seek safety from the plague in

Jena. His friend, Dr. Bugenhagen, and a few others remained with Luther, and shared with him the dangers of his post. In a letter to a friend, at this time, he says: "I am not alone; because the Lord Christ, the prayers of saints, and the angelic host, though invisible, are with us in power and great number." During the prevalence of the plague, Luther also wrote a little work entitled, "Answer to the Question, 'Ought we to be Afraid to Die?'"

But the bitterest experience of Luther's tender and sympathetic heart during this troublous year, was the news he constantly received of the martyr death of many of his steadfast friends of the purified Church, "followers of the true faith and Luther's doctrines," as they loved to call themselves, who were forced to seal their devotion by cruel deaths at the hands of the Papists, as "contumacious heretics." This was notably the case in Bavaria. Prominent among these martyred heroes was Luther's personal friend, Leonard Kaiser, Vicar of Watzenkirchen, who was burned at the stake by order of the Pope, at Scherding, near Passau, August 16, 1527. Luther wrote to the condemned man a characteristic letter, full of deep feeling, heavenly hope, and spiritual power, and, in addition, tried every available means to save the life of his doomed friend, but in vain. He was sacrificed upon the bloody altar of hate and religious fanaticism.

After Kaiser had been put to death, Luther wrote to a friend of the victim: "O, that I were as worthy to overcome Satan and pass out of this world as did our dear murdered friend! Glory to God, who hath given to our unworthy selves these beautiful examples of his grace! Kaiser has risen triumphant over the Prince of Darkness, and has even subjugated Death by his most glorious victory!" In another letter, dated November the first, of the same year, Luther writes to a friend, "This is the tenth anniversary of the victory over the Pope's absolution humbug, and we are even at this moment appropriately celebrating that event." Luther closes the letter as follows: "So, then, we have war without and war within; but Christ Jesus is with us. Our greatest consolation, and which we effectually oppose to the wrath of the powers of hell, is, that we have the Word of God, which saveth the soul even though the body be swallowed and destroyed in the devices of Satan. Pray for us, that we may continue to bear stoutly the cross of the Lord, and that we may conquer Satan, and destroy his designs, either by life or by death. Amen!"

Even as the martyr death of two other young followers of Luther, the monks Henry Voes and John Esch, at Brussels, July 1, 1523, inspired him to compose his first grand pean of the Reformation, beginning "A new Song to the Lord we Sing," so the trials and painful experiences of the year 1527, doubtless, inspired the celestial muse of Luther to compose that grand and divinely heroic battle-hymn of the Reformation, "Eine feste Burg ist unser Gott," whose imperishable strains, whether heard in the din and roar of battle or floating out upon the solemn Sabbath air from village church or peasant's cot, have never failed to inspire the soul of the Christian with the most fervid emotions of religious enthusiasm. Luther found great consolation and much of his poetic inspiration in the majestic and inspired Psalms of David. He knew them by heart, and always loved to quote from the music of this sacred Harp of Israel. The hymn alluded to above, "Eine feste Burg," etc., is founded upon the Psalm xlvi: "God is our refuge and strength, a very present help in trouble;" and in praise of his favorite Psalm (cxviii) Luther speaks in the most affectionate terms, even in his poetic fervor going so far as to personify it, thus: "Often and most faithfully hath he stood by me, and released me from many a profound affliction when neither emperor, king, sage, saint, or philosopher could have helped me; therefore, he is dearer to me than all the wealth, honor, and power of the world."

How deeply he was imbued with the olden spirit of the apostolic age, is apparent in another letter to a friend, in which Luther says: "My enemies have striven by every means in their power to shake my purpose, and to extirpate me and mine, root and branch; but, nevertheless, the Lord preserved me from the effects of their evil designs, and kept them within bounds. They never could carry out their wickedness. They can push, but not overthrow. They can torment, but not destroy. They can torture, but can not force. They can embarrass, but not prevent. They can show their teeth, but not devour. They can murder, burn, hang, and drown, but they can not quench the spirit. They can rob, expel, and confiscate, but they can not seal the mouth of the people. In short, they can do a little, but they can not fulfill their heart's desire. 'The Lord is my helper.' Who is it that can harm those whom the Lord protects? Remember, the Word of the Lord endureth forever."

Luther was a Christian hero in the apostolic sense; thoroughly filled with the sublime spirit of David, Elias, and Moses; always rising victorious from defeat, and stronger in soul from every humiliation. All his plans and theories were founded upon what he says about his own work in a letter still extant: "I built my cause upon the written Word of God. With this Word, and by the aid and grace of Heaven, I have carried out my plan thus far; with this Word I have overcome all of my foes; upon this Word I still survive and stand, and upon this Word will I go, through death, to my blessed Lord and Redeemer. Therefore, whoever would stand by the side of Christ and assist me in destroying the enemies of God, let him come."

Prayer was the great anchor of his hope, the

celestial balm for every wound, the solace of his darkest hours, and the joy of his brightest.

Speaking of Luther's character in this respect, a former servant of his exclaims: "How great was the faith, how lovely the spirit of his words! I once had the happiness of hearing him pray, and it seemed to me as if it was a child fervently talking to a loving parent," etc. This person further states that Luther devoted a large portion of his time daily to prayer, never less than three hours.

In 1532, Luther was much afflicted with vertigo, which his physicians looked upon as premonitory symptoms of apoplexy. In 1536, he was confined to his bed for a long time with severe neuralgia. In 1537, while attending a convention of the Church, he was attacked with a painful disease of the bladder, which grew worse so rapidly that his death was hourly expected; and Luther prepared his last will and testament. He recovered as by a miracle, but during the few years which the Lord still vouchsafed him on earth he was continually struggling with debility and disease.

Still, in his eagerness to serve God, and in his desire to rescue his maltreated Church from the foul grasp of the Roman hierarchy, he could not deprive himself of the pleasure of devoting the ebbing moments of his laborious life to the vigorous defense of his cause against the persistent and unscrupulous assaults of his priestly enemies. In the years 1535, 36, 38, and 40, he labored upon and published revised editions of his German Bible. In 1541, another edition, most carefully revised by Luther and his most learned friends, appeared. This last passed through many editions, and received the finishing revisory touches of Luther's pen in 1545. This edition may be considered the normal German Bible, being the authorized and acknowledged Bible now in use in all the Protestant Churches of Germany.

In 1543, Luther was conscious of such a

decrease in physical strength and of his approaching dissolution, that, in a letter to a friend, he writes: "Pray for me, that I may die in peace; for I have finished the labor of my life, and the end is near. 'We would have healed Babylon, but she is not healed; forsake her.' (Jeremiah li, 9.)"

Faithfully, however, did Luther continue to teach the living Word in sermons that had lost none of their force and beauty by reason of his bodily decay. Whenever his debility prevented him from filling his pulpit, he would preach at his own house to large and devout congregations. In this manner he preached up to the evening preceding the day of his death. All of these sermons were collected and published in a large volume in 1544. The heavenly fount of Poesie never failed in his heart, but retained its freshness and purity to the last. Still he wrote and composed the music to admirable devotional hymns, full of celestial fire, and rich with thought and poetic grace. Thirty-seven of these beautiful hymns are still sung with fervent appreciation by the Protestant congregations of the German Empire.

These sacred songs, like winged evangels, proceeded from Luther's inspired pen, and visited every nook and cranny of the German realm; nor could anathemas or solemn decrees from ecclesiastical tribunals stay their glorious flight. On the lips of wandering "tramps," in the rude music of the mountain shepherd, or cheering the labor of the brawny peasant upon the harvest-field, these sacred strains perpetuated themselves, and became part and parcel of the German heart. It was often the case, too, that when some strolling monk or servile priest attempted to preach from the pulpit, in the rural districts, the worn-out and corrupt doctrines of the old Church, his whole congregation would commence to chant, in sweet unison, one of Luther's grand and inspiring hymns, effectually drowning the blasphemous words of the disgusted disciple of Roman superstition; washing him and his pollution, as it were, completely out of the holy precincts upon the mighty and swelling floods of Christian melody.

CHAPTER XVI.

THE DEATH OF LUTHER—HIS FUNERAL—SCENES AND INCIDENTS.

ON the 28th of January, 1546, Luther arrived at Eisleben, where he had gone, in spite of his feeble condition of health, in order to act as arbitrator in a difficulty into which his friend, the Earl of Mansfield, had fallen. During the entire period of three weeks which Luther was compelled to devote to this case, he felt extremely ill, and on the 17th of February he grew so much worse, that it was evident to all, as well as to himself, that his end had come. It was on this day that Luther wrote his last beautiful and well-known prayer: "My dear and heavenly Father! thou God and Father of our Lord Jesus Christ! thou God of truth! I thank thee that thou hast declared unto me thy beloved Son, Christ Jesus; in whom I believe, whom I have preached and acknowledged before all men; whom I have loved and defended; but whom the wicked Pope and his ungodly followers defame and persecute. I pray, Lord Jesus Christ, that thou wilt take my soul into thy gracious keeping. And O, my heavenly Father! although I must lay off this body, and am to be taken out of this life, still I know that I am to remain with thee for evermore, and that out of thy sacred hands nothing can take me. Receive and accept, O heavenly Father, my thanks for thy everlasting love and mercy, for Christ's sake. Amen."

When Luther had finished, in a calm, firm voice, the recitation of this prayer, he from time to time prayed in the Latin tongue; and quoted passages from the Scriptures in the same language. Some one at his bedside offered him some tonic medicines; but he gently declined to take it, saying, "I am going; my spirit is ready to receive its eternal rest." A few moments later he ejaculated thrice, in rapid succession, the words: "Father, into thy hands I commend my soul! Dear Lord and Master, thou art my salvation!"

Just before the illustrious spirit fled from its mortal body, Dr. Jonas, who was standing close to him, bent over the side of the bed, and said to Luther:

"Reverend father, are you willing to die in Christ and the doctrine as you have preached it to the world?"

Luther, in a clear voice, audible to all within the room, replied, "Yes." Then, drawing a deep breath, he expired, his hands folded upon his breast, without a sign of pain or tremor of death upon his placid features. Sweetly, tranquilly, as an infant drops into slumber upon the bosom of its mother, Luther sank into the arms of the waiting angels; hopefully, gloriously, his mighty spirit divested itself from the grievous shackles of mortality, and soared to the realms of immortal bliss. His death, as his life, in calm simplicity and the deathless grandeur of spiritual heroism, added to the records of the world's history one of its most charming pages, and placed in the zenith of the dark Past one of its fairest and most refulgent stars. "Verily, verily, I say unto you, if a man keep my saying, he shall never see death."

It was Thursday morning, about three o'clock, February 18, 1546, when Luther, the great Reformer, passed from earth to immortality. Let the memory of this day be kept fresh and hallowed in the hearts of all true Christians.

Rarely did the death of any man create profounder sorrow among a people than did that of Luther among his countrymen, and wherever his name had become familiar throughout

Christendom. Rev. Dr. Jonas, his tried and intimate friend, preached his funeral sermon in the Church of St. Andrew, in Eisleben, on the 19th. Luther's remains were thence taken to Halle on the 21st; from thence to Kemberg; and on the 22d of February they arrived at Wittenberg. All along the route of the funeral procession the church-bells tolled their sad requiem over the dust of the illustrious dead, and vast multitudes of people from all sections of the country thronged to see it, and, weeping, followed the imposing cortege. In the town of Halle the scene was peculiarly impressive; and in Wittenberg the entire population turned out to receive the beloved ashes of their father and friend, and escort them to their final resting-place. Rev. Dr. Bugenhagen, who preached the sermon in the old cathedral, was repeatedly forced to stop in the delivery of his discourse, overcome by his own emotions and the loud weeping of the multitude gathered under the sacred roof to pay their last tribute to the memory of Luther. Melanchthon, so deeply affected that his voice was scarcely audible, closed the solemn services and pronounced the benediction, whereupon the coffin was lowered into its destined vault in the immediate vicinity of the altar.

Thus was the champion of God's truth, and the standard-bearer of a new era of religious faith, taken from the world; but the fruit of his labor and the splendor of his priceless victories remain. Luther, doubtless, was the greatest evangelist and most successful successor of the apostles that the world has produced since the close of the apostolic age,— like John, in his reverence and love for the Master; like Peter, fervent and prompt in action; like Paul, learned, and profound in thought. Like David, he spared not, in word or deed, the foes of his God; and the boldness and power of his tongue equaled the burning eloquence of Elias. He combined, in one person, the "speaker of tongues" and interpreter of holy things, the prophet and the evangelist.

Filled with every gift of grace; a burning and a shining light; a pillar of the Church militant; the prototype of a Christian husband, father, and friend, in his domestic relations; a master of the German language; a man simple, humble, and upright in all things; unsophisticated as a child, yet profoundly versed in the lore of the world; indefatigable in the planning and accomplishment of great works, yet always giving God and his Redeemer the honor and the praise; persecuted, reviled, mocked, and despised, yet ever cheerful and resigned; poor, yet making many rich,—ever blessed be the memory of this great and good man!

CHAPTER XVII.

REMINISCENSES OF WARTBURG AND WITTENBERG.

THE Wartburg, the scene of Luther's captivity, is one of the most beautiful and romantically situated of all the old German castles. It is now an appendage of the Grand Ducal Crown of Weimar, and a grand center of attraction to tourists and antiquarians from all parts of the world. Overlooking the gray walls and quaint steeples of the old town of Eisenach and a vast stretch of landscape which, for picturesque beauty and diversified natural attractions, is unexcelled in all the German Empire, the Wartburg holds fast to its proud station in the esteem of the citizens of the Father-land. Legendary lore and the magic of song has wreathed the old mountain fortress with perennial flowers; but the fact that over three centuries ago it was the asylum of the great Reformer, Martin Luther, his "island of Patmos," his "eyrie," and "hermitage," as he delights in calling his place of refuge, adds a brighter effulgence to the history of these stalwart towers, and hallows it as the Mecca of Germany. The Wartburg, under the auspices of the present Grand Duke of Weimar, was restored to its pristine magnificence; this labor of love and reverence having been completed but a few years ago. All that industry and art could accomplish has been lavished upon the splendid edifice, and, like a phœnix risen from the dust and ashes of decay, the Wartburg, in every essential particular, rejoices to-day in all its ancient glory.

Luther, while living in the castle, resided in what is called the "Ritterhaus." Here the little apartment he occupied can be seen, not precisely as he left it when he escaped to Wittenberg, but still in a remarkable state of preservation, it being evident that the architect in charge of the general restoration of the edifice devoted the most scrupulous attention to this sanctuary. The massive oaken table upon which Luther began his translation of the Bible has long ago disappeared, chipped into myriad fragments by the knives of reckless relic-hunters; but in its place now stands the one at which Luther was wont to sit in the parental homestead at Moehra. The bed in which he slept while stopping over night in Castle Gleisen, and a table from the room he there occupied, are also placed in the Wartburg room. The stove, almost as huge as a baker's oven, and which used to cheer the musing monk with its grateful warmth, also stands, in its original vastness, in a corner of the apartment, the pieces of "kachel" of which it is composed having been dug out of the accumulated rubbish of the ruin. The walls are adorned with a portrait of Luther, from the celebrated brush of his intimate friend and contemporary, Lukas Cranach, as well as portraits of his parents. An autograph letter of Luther's, in a handsome frame, hangs opposite the door. On a small book-case, filled with various editions of the Bible, is to be seen the miner's lamp of Luther's father, and to the right of this the little, well-worn money-box carried by Luther around the streets of Eisenach in his capacity as a mendicant chorister. A fragment of the vertebra of a whale, lying upon the floor, is said to have been used by Luther as a footstool. Upon the wall, in close proximity of the huge stove, is to be seen the celebrated "ink-spot," the dark memento of his marvelous encounter with the Prince of Evil.

No less interesting are the souvenirs of the Reformer to be seen at Wittenberg; and hundreds make pilgrimages to this shrine of Protestantism annually. An American tourist, who recently visited the place, describes in a graphic manner some of the most historic mementos still preserved in the venerable burgh.

"Wittenberg still keeps its ancient walls, but, with its rather diminished population, still affords ample room for all her children. Approaching the gate from the railway station, we notice on our right a young oak surrounded by a high fence, inside of which bushes and dead stalks of last Summer's flowers are standing up through the snow, while outside are benches and a flower-garden. On this spot Luther burned the Papal Bull. In order to assist the imagination of visitors to the historic spot, a small quantity of ashes are commonly kept upon it.

"We pass through the low, thick portal, pass crookedly to the left, and find ourselves in the principal street of the city. On the way to the chief hotel we pass Melanchthon's house and the University. Retracing our steps from the hotel, we come to the Augusteum, or ancient domicile of the Augustine monks, the order to which Luther belonged. It is three stories high, gray with mortar and age, and has two rows of windows set in its long, retiring roof, that look down upon you like magnified human eyes. On the opposite side of the court stands the abode of the Reformer. Before climbing up the narrow flight of stairs, the guide points out a curiously wrought door-casing, done in stone, and says that Mrs. Luther had this put up during her husband's absence as a surprise gift for him on his return. We enter, and go up to the second floor. The stairs are old, the ante-room bleak and gloomy, and as fast as possible we press into the rooms of Luther. These are two, a large and a small one, but both are high. The larger one is where he worked and lived with his soft-eyed wife. The thick walls furnish spacious window-seats. Beside one of these, stands an odd-looking seat, which he used in his studies. It is plain and narrow. I thought at first that a man of Luther's size would hardly find it roomy enough; but when the largest of our party sat down in it, my doubts vanished. The guide declared that Luther and his wife used to sit together in its arms. If this was so, the pretty 'Frau Doctor' must have been on her husband's knee or in his arms when they accomplished that feat. The floor is very old. Its softer portions having been worn away, the tougher knots stand out very prominently. In one corner is a huge stove, such as would heat a church in America, but which are in common use in German households. This stove was made in Eisenach, and was a gift from its citizens to the great preacher. On it are figures of the four evangelists, and other ornaments. The heavy table in the center of the room is a relic of the days of the Reformation, and you can easily fancy a noble group of the good and great men of those times leaning over it in deep and earnest conversation. Ah, if it could only speak! On the walls hang portraits of Luther, and a colored cast of his face taken after death. It is a pity that there is no portrait of Catherine, his gentle and beloved wife. Here, as at Eisenach, is a huge mug whence he quaffed his beer. One might easily suppose that he was a greedy drinker as he looks at these, and such an idea has a seeming confirmation in his well-known couplet:

> 'Who loves not woman, wine, and song,
> Remains a fool his whole life long.'

Of this and many other sins his enemies have accused him; but it is needless to say that these stories are simply falsehoods. When we consider what a diligent toiler, in so many various ways, the Reformer was, we shall hardly find it possible that it should have been otherwise. The autograph of Peter the Great, carefully protected by a glass, is the only other relic in this room, and is an object of nearly as much interest as any thing else there. In the sleeping-room there are samplers wrought by the hands of Catherine, autographs of Luther, and other smaller articles in a kind of secretary. And this is all there is to see. The rest of the rooms on this floor are vacant and dull.

"The University was transferred to Halle fifty years ago, and united with another there.

"We pass out, and listen for a moment to the plash of the little fountain in the court, where Luther must have often quenched his thirst, and listened to the soothing melody of the silvery flood. We are again in the street. We are taking the same walk which Luther himself once took under very different circumstances. As we go along we seem to see the stout form of that courageous servant of God moving on before us, bent upon breaking forever the chains of ancient error, and to open anew for the world long-sealed fountains of truth. His mind had been made up, his invincible will fixed, and the light of Heaven was shining on this path as Luther wended his way to Wittenberg church, for the purpose of nailing his sublime 'Theses' against its portal, so that all the world might read. One almost fancies himself humming, unconsciously, his own valiant words as we approach the spot:

> 'A mighty fortress is our God,
> A good defense and weapon.'

"We have completed the walk, and stand facing the doors of the 'Schloss Kirche.' It was here that the famous 'Theses' were nailed up by Luther's own energetic hand; but not on this very door, where so fine a copy of them stands. The French burned a former copy, and with it the ancient doors. The present ones are of bronze, and are a gift from the Prussian Crown. Entering the church, we notice its long, narrow, and high aspect, with its ends rounding off like those of an ellipse. It looks clean and well kept. In the middle of the church, and near the door, are the graves of Melanchthon and his greater friend standing in the middle of the central isle, just where it is intersected by that which comes from the door. As you face the altar, Luther's grave will be on your right, Melanchthon's on your left. Large slabs of marble tell, in few words, who slumber beneath them. The church is not remarkable in itself. We step into the chancel, and reflect that Luther was often there; we ascend the pulpit, and hear the guide declare that there Melanchthon once became confused in the midst of the sermon, and was forced to break off abruptly, whereupon Luther, who was sitting among the audience, arose with a smile, saying, 'Come down, innocent lamb, and let me preach.' He mounted the pulpit vacated by his diffident friend, and thrilled the congregation with one of his most perfect and powerful sermons. But, after all, the center of attraction is by the two graves. We go back, talk and linger about them, and finally lingeringly depart.

The church is open every Sunday for divine worship, and, the guide assures us, is thronged.

"We return to the market-place, and curiously examine the statues of the immortal dead as they stand together there. These are of bronze, and are quite characteristic. Both are represented in their academical robes. Luther's features are roughly kind in their expression. On the pedestals are several of his pregnant sayings; as, 'If it be God's work, it will stand; if it be man's work, it will perish;' 'Our God is a strong tower,' etc. The head of Melanchthon is fine and massive. Most of the pictures of him are devoid of expression; but there is a drawing in the Royal Library, at Berlin, wherein his face shows great vivacity and force. It is by Cranach. The splendid personal qualities of Luther have won him a brighter fame than his friend's. There is, perhaps, no more striking example of the superiority of character to great acquirements than this. In subtilty of mind, extent of learning, and patience, Melanchthon was doubtless superior to the other. But Luther was much more in sympathy with his time. He had also the gift of setting his valiant thoughts in sonorous hymns. Besides this was his rare art of coining his brave ideas and witty fancies into striking proverbs—the ready money of popular thinking. Now, he who is always on the lips of men in proverb or song can never be far from their hearts. Luther is alive all over Germany to-day, and Melanchthon is remembered chiefly as his friend.

"We are musing long over these men; and yet we should care little for the town but for them. Their magnetic names drew our feet hither, and render it hard for them to depart. It would be sad, indeed, if we should fail to recognize that the grace of God made these Reformers great, or that duty, done at all hazards, is the only straight road to true fame and everlasting peace. This, especially, is the grand lesson of Luther's life."

THE LUTHER MONUMENT AT WORMS.

(CENTRAL FIGURE.)

CHAPTER XVIII.

THE LUTHER MONUMENT IN WORMS.

WORMS, the venerable and ancient city around whose history the memory of Luther has thrown its own halo of consecrated light, has of late become still more attractive to the intelligent traveler in Europe, by reason of the monument erected to the great Reformer in one of the public squares of the old imperial city. A minute description of this beautiful work of art may not prove altogether uninteresting.

The whole monument rests upon a quadrangular sub-structure of granite, each side of which measures forty feet. At each of the four corners of this massive foundation, upon pedestals of finely polished syenite eight feet in height, stands the bronze statue, eight feet high, of one of the most eminent and influential supporters and promoters of the Reformation. Facing to the front, on the left-hand side, is Frederick the Wise, Elector of Saxony; upon the right-hand is Philip the Magnanimous, Landgrave of Hessia; on the rear corner, behind Philip, but also facing in the same direction, stands Philip Melanchthon; and opposite, behind the Elector Frederick, is John Reuchlin. The front of the quadrangle is open, forming an entrance thirty feet wide, between the statues of Philip of Hessia and Frederick of Saxony, into the interior space.

The other three sides of the square, however, are inclosed by an embrasured wall of polished syenite, between four and five feet in height. Out of the center of each of these walls, upon a seven-foot pedestal of syenite, and in a reclining posture, rests the figure of a female, each of them six feet in height, and emblematical of the three chief Protestant cities of the Reformation,—Augsburg, with a palm-branch in her hand, in sign of peace; Magdeburg, in deep mourning; and the protesting Spire. Upon the inner face of the twenty-four embrasures appear the coat-of-arms of each of the twenty-four cities which fought and suffered in the cause of the Reformation, namely: Brunswick, Bremen, Constance, Eisenach, Eisleben, Emden, Erfurt, Frankfort-on-the-Main, Suabian Halle, Hamburg, Heilbronn, Jena, Königsberg, Leipzic, Lindau, Lübeck, Marburg, Memmingen, Nördlingen, Riga, Schmalkalden, Strasberg, Ulm, and Wittenberg.

From the center of the surroundings just described rises the Luther monument proper. Upon the four abutting socles of the sixteen feet high and richly ornamented main pedestal, are seated four venerated pioneers of the Reformation, namely: the Frank, Petrus Waldus, died 1197; the Englishman, John Wyclif, died 1387; the Bohemian, John Huss, died 1415; and the Italian, Hieronymus Savonarola, died 1492. Towering in stately beauty over all, and, as it were, crowning the magnificent whole, stands the colossal bronze statue of Luther, ten and a half feet in height, the entire column, including the pedestal, reaching an altitude of twenty-seven feet.

The main pedestal consists of three parts— the socle of polished syenite, the upper and lower cube, of unequal breadth and height, and composed of bronze. On each of the four sides of the upper cube is inscribed some familiar maxim of Luther's, or trenchant quotation from his writings, as well as two medallion portraits of distinguished contemporaries and participants in the cause of the Reformation.

On the front side, immediately under the base of Luther's statue, are to be seen those brave and decisive words of his, uttered in this very place: "Here I stand; I can not do otherwise. God help me! Amen." Below these lines appear the portraits of the two Saxon Electors, John the Firm, and John Frederick the Magnanimous; the former to the left, the latter to the right of the observer. Upon the rear side of this cap-cube appears this passage from one of his tracts: "The Gospel, which the Lord gave into the mouth of the apostles, is his sword, with which, as with a thunderbolt, he cleaveth the world." Under these lines are the portraits of those valiant knights and warriors, Ulrich von Hutten and Francis von Sickingen; the former to the left, the latter to the right of the observer. Upon the side, to the right of Luther, we find two of Luther's aphorisms: "Faith means a righteous and true life in God;" and, "Truthfully to comprehend the Scriptures requires the Spirit of Christ." Under these lines are the portraits of Luther's faithful companions and colaborers in the work, Justus Jonas and John

Bugenhagen; the former to the left, the latter to the right of the observer. On the side to the left of Luther are the words: "Whosoever understandeth Christ can never be held captive by the false statutes of man; they are free, not carnally, but in spirit and conscience." Under this quotation are the portraits of the two Swiss Reformers, John Calvin and Ulrich Zwingle; the former to the left, the latter to the right of the observer.

The lower cube of the main pedestal is ornamented with sculpture in *basso-relievo*, representing some of the most interesting incidents in the life of Luther. On the front face is Luther before the Imperial Diet at Worms, April 17, 18, 1521. On the rear face is Luther nailing his THESES against the church door in Wittenberg, October 31, 1517. To the right of his statue is Luther administering the Lord's-supper, and Luther's wedding. To the left is the Bible translation, and Luther preaching.

The substructure, or socle, shows upon its four sides the coat-of-arms of the five German sovereigns and two cities who signed the Confession of Augsburg, and formally presented the memorable document to the emperor, at the Diet held in Augsburg June 25, 1530; namely, Saxony, Anhalt, Brandenburg, Hessia, Brunswick-Lüneburg, and the cities of Nuremberg and Reutlingen. Upon the broad belt encircling the base of the pedestal under the bas-reliefs is the following inscription: "Begun A. D. 1836. Finished A. D. 1868. Designed and in part completed by E. Rietschel. Architectural designs by H. Nicolai. Cast and enchased at Lauchhammer."

Rietschel, the famous sculptor, who died February 21, 1861, himself modeled the statues of Luther and Wycklif, while three pupils of this renowned master—Donndorf, Kietz, and Schilling—furnished the models for the remaining statues and bas-reliefs. The massive granite work was done at Baireuth.

The entire square in which the monument is situated is inclosed with a handsomely ornamented iron railing.

The idea of a Luther monument sprang spontaneously from the loyal heart of the German people; and the fund to defray the cost of its erection was contributed from every city, town, village, and hamlet throughout the German Father-land. It is a nation's memorial tribute to one of its greatest benefactors and most illustrious children. In point of art it stands unexcelled by any similar work of ancient or modern times, and is certainly the most costly and magnificent public monument in Germany, and in every way worthy of the genius and patriotism of its people.

The inauguration of the monument, and the festivities incident to the occasion, took place during the 24th, 25th, and 26th days of June, 1868. For impressiveness, grandeur, and enthusiasm, the affair has never been excelled, and thousands of curious visitors from all parts of the world were attracted to the scene. Those who were present will remember the inauguration of the Luther Monument in Worms as one of the grandest demonstrations of modern times. The city, which is three-fourths Catholic, was overwhelmed by a visitation of one hundred thousand people, and had to overflow into all the neighboring towns and villages, after taxing its own hospitality to the utmost. The German enthusiasm for the great hero fairly obliterated for the time the distinction of Catholic and Protestant, and all joined in doing honor to a man who is universally recognized, not only as the author of the Reformation, but as the father of German literature, and one of the grandest spirits of modern times.

The King of Prussia took the leading part in the ceremonies, assisted by princes and eminent men from all parts of Europe. When the monument was delivered to the city authorities, it was a Catholic Mayor who represented the city, and accepted the national gift in its behalf. His speech was a singular proof how much the spirit of strife and animosity yielded to humane and national considerations on this auspicious occasion. It commemorated, in the most striking and eloquent terms, the services which Luther's moral courage and genius rendered to the German race and to mankind, when he stood upon his right of conscience before the emperor and the Papal power, and declared that he could not and would not retract the principles of religious freedom and reform which he inculcated, and in defense of which he was willing to offer his life as a sacrifice.

All honor to Germany for this public evidence of the catholicity of spirit which so notably pervades its glorious people, and which, we trust, will prove the happy augury of the near approach of that anxiously expected time, when Christendom, in undivided phalanx, shall triumph over the enemies of God wherever found, and in heavenly harmony shall together sing the *gloria* anthem of Universal Peace.

As for Luther, and the fruitful and splendid lessons of his life, emblemized in the rare bronze and stone of the Worms Monument, we can say, in the beautiful language of the poet, that he became

> "A name Earth wears forever next her heart;
> One of the few that have a right to rank
> With the true makers; for his spirit wrought
> Order from Chaos; proved that right divine
> Dwelt only in the excellence of **Truth**;
> And far within old Darkness' hostile lines
> Advanced and pitched the shining tents of Light."

www.ingramcontent.com/pod-product-compliance
Lightning Source LLC
Chambersburg PA
CBHW030256170426
43202CB00009B/766